Bring Your Own GOD

The Spirituality of Woody Guthrie

Rev. Steve Edington

And

Woody Guthrie

Order this book online at www.trafford.com
or email orders@trafford.com

Most Trafford titles are also available at major online book retailers.

Foreword by Ellis Paul
Cover design by Richard Widhu
Author photo by Dan Murphy

Printed in the United States of America.

ISBN: 978-1-4669-4447-3 (sc)
ISBN: 978-1-4669-4448-0 (e)

Trafford rev. *07/21/2012*

 www.trafford.com

North America & international
toll-free: 1 888 232 4444 (USA & Canada)
phone: 250 383 6864 ♦ fax: 812 355 4082

PERMISSIONS AND CREDITS

CONTENTS

Preface and Acknowledgements

*T*his is the fourth book I've written that calls for a fair amount of research; and then there's the matter of taking the research and creating a narrative out of it. It can be a tedious task at times. But the joy of such an undertaking is found in meeting some wonderful people who share your interests and passions, and who encourage you on your way. That has certainly proven to be the case with this book. The thoughts I offer now that it's completed are interwoven with a lot of gratitude for a lot of kind and helpful folks.

My first word of thanks goes to a man I never met, Woody Guthrie himself. I thank him for documenting—in letters, songs, poems, journals, song commentaries, or just plain scribblings—so much of his far flung, wide ranging life. For a man who spent a goodly portion of his life on the move and on the road, Woody still took the time to do an amazing amount of writing. His writings took on an especially poignant and courageous dimension in the early-to-mid 1950s as his series of hospitalizations for Huntington's Disease got underway.

Well before that decade was over he would no longer be able to put pen or pencil to paper as his deterioration from Huntington's progressed. But until that time arrived he poured forth some of the deepest reaches of his soul, as he reached for some of the deepest wellsprings of spiritual sustenance that he could find. It was these writings in particular that help me to uncover much of the spirituality of Woody Guthrie. Without his willingness and ability to open up some of the most personal regions of his life, much of the spiritual side of Woody would have remained hidden.

The writings of an individual like Woody Guthrie, however, are only as valuable as they are preserved and made available. Recognizing this, I offer a tremendous word of thanks and appreciation to the Woody Guthrie Foundation and Archives for their great job of maintaining and cataloguing so much of what Woody produced. Archivist Tiffany Colannino was especially helpful and cooperative during my visits to the Foundation in Mt. Kisco, New York. Not only did she make available every item from the Archive I requested, she also became familiar enough with the nature of my research that she located several items for me that I would not have found on my own. She also put me in touch with other scholars who have a similar interest in this dimension of Woody's life as I do. Thanks, Tiffany.

Anna Canoni, a grand-daughter of Woody's, worked with me on the various licensing and permission matters that need to be dealt with in order for a work such as this one to get published. I've enjoyed working with her. Thanks, Anna.

I am particularly appreciative as well of the Board of Directors of the Guthrie Foundation and Archives, in conjunction with the BMI Foundation, for giving me a research grant to help support my work.

Finally, along this line, I am grateful that the WG Foundation and Archives in Mt. Kisco are located at a reasonable driving distance from my home in southern New Hampshire. In 2013 the Archive is being moved to Tulsa, Oklahoma—not far from Woody's hometown of Okemah—with the support of the George Kaiser Family Foundation. I think it's wonderful that Woody's works are coming to his home state. And I'm glad I got my research done before they left New York!

I probably would not have even embarked upon this project were it not for the initial urging and encouragement of my friend from Lowell, Massachusetts, Jimmy Pollard. Jimmy is one of the mainstays of the annual Woody Guthrie Festivals in Okemah. I first met him through my long time involvement in the Lowell Celebrates Kerouac Committee, as he joined his connection with Woody Guthrie to his appreciation for Lowell native, Jack Kerouac. Jimmy was aware of my explorations into the religion and spirituality of some of the Beat Generation writers, and he was the one who first pushed me to do some similar explorations with Woody Guthrie. He also provided me with some of the harder to get published works of Woody's, as well as his labor-of-love transcription of Woody's unpublished play *Forsaken Bibel*. Thanks so much, Jimmy.

As noted at the outset, the great joy of undertaking a project like this one are the human connections one makes in pursuing it. My longtime friendship with musician, composer, and author David Amram took on yet another dimension with our shared interest in Woody Guthrie. I was honored to have attended one of the early concert performances, in New York City, of David's *Symphonic Variations on a Song by Woody Guthrie*. I thank David both for all the support he's given me in my Beat Generation pursuits, and now for my delving into Woody's spirituality. I'm especially grateful for his kind and generous words on the back jacket of this book.

Another gentleman who is very well versed in all things Woody is Barry Ollman of Denver, Colorado. He and I have touched base on occasion as my work took shape; and I thank him for his words of support and encouragement.

Two other musicians who have a great appreciation for Woody's work and who have set some of his writings to music they have composed are Joel Rafael and Jimmy LaFave. I appreciate the interest each of these gentlemen have shown in my work, and for the personal support they have given me.

Still another musician who has brought some of Woody's previously unknown writings to light is Ellis Paul, the song *God's Promise* in particular. Ellis spent some time with me before one of his concerts in the Boston area in the spring of 2011, as we shared some of our mutual interests in Woody's work. He has written a very fine Foreword to the text I've written. Thank you, Ellis Paul.

In thinking of all people I've met and talked with in the course of creating this work, there are two individuals who especially stand out. They are Guy Logsdon and Mary Jo Guthrie Edgmon. Guy Logsdon is a fellow Oklahoman of Woody's and is extremely well versed in his life. Like Jimmy Pollard, he's one of the regulars at the annual WoodyFests in Okemah, and he was very generous with his time spent with me for an interview in Okemah in 2011. I am honored to have his commentary on the back jacket of this book.

I don't know when I've encountered a more delightful and positive spirited person than Woody's sister, Mary Jo Guthrie Edgmon. If I manage to make it to the age of 90, as she has, I can only hope that I do so with her attitude and spirit! She and I had a brief meet-up at the 2011 WoodyFest; and our subsequent telephone conversations from the care facility where she now resides in Shawnee, Oklahoma—which she calls her "country club"—always make my day. I especially thank her for the insights she's given me on Woody's early religious influences, as you'll read in the pages ahead; and for her kind and generous words on the back cover of this book. May Mary Jo continue to live long and well!

Closer to home I thank my congregation at the Unitarian Universalist Church of Nashua, New Hampshire. After 24 years, my ministry with them closes in the summer of 2012. I'm grateful for the space they've given me to write this book and for the interest they have shown in my Woody explorations. Two individuals in my congregation who have helped contribute to this work are Richard Widhu who designed the book cover; and Dan Murphy—a fellow Woody aficionado—who took the author photo. I also thank my sister Rose Edington for her great assistance in making textual corrections.

For all of the help and good wishes I've had from so many people, my greatest single piece of inspiration came in a brief telephone conversation with Nora Guthrie shortly after I first contacted the Guthrie Foundation about doing a research and writing project about Woody Guthrie's religious roots, and the sources of his spirituality. Her words to me were, "This is a piece of Woody's life that is sitting there waiting for someone to pick up."

I didn't realize just how much was "sitting there" until I began to dig into the material; and I haven't come close to picking up all the pieces that make up the spiritual mosaic of Woody Guthrie's life. For every piece of archival material that I copied down, or had photocopied, there were so many other pieces that I had to leave sitting there. I hope that what I have been able to uncover and record in the chapters ahead will offer a good and representative sample of Woody Guthrie's spiritual life, and of the very wide range of religious thought and expression he drew upon in shaping his own philosophy of life.

My additional hope is to get a conversation going about the breadth, depth, and full meaning of Woody's remark to his friend Jim Longhi that he (Woody) did consider himself a religious man and that he had a liking for all of the world's faiths. For those who wish to join that conversation there is still plenty of material yet to be perused, and much more of Woody's spiritual life to be brought to light. So, pick it up!

Stephen Edington
Nashua, New Hampshire
June, 2012

FOREWORD

By Ellis Paul

Woody Guthrie carved out a path of understanding through his life with songs, and he wrote thousands of them. The popular notion of his writing is that he was a musical spokesman for the working man. This is a fair tag, mainly because the songs he did make known to the world possessed a power that grew into rallying cries for workers' rights and labor unions.

But what of the thousands of song he had written that were lesser known, even unpublished and unrecorded?

The genre range of his complete works is as broad as life itself: Children's songs, bawdy songs, anti-war songs, pro-war songs, angry songs, satirical songs; and yes, songs about God, religion, and spirituality.

This work, now completed by Steve Edington, is a much needed, and thoughtfully researched look at Woody's life and the songs of spirituality he wrote, and why he wrote them. I'm thrilled that it will help more people see Woody as a three dimensional artist and human being who was leading a self-made spiritual journey through life, as he was guided by adventures, art, relationships, tragedy and longing. God was there with him, and makes appearances in the numerous songs which Steve has so thoughtfully presented. I like Woody's God. It's the God I'm seeking as well.

CHAPTER ONE

The Church of Woody?

The building was immortalized in the late 1960s and early 70s by Arlo Guthrie when it was the home of Alice and Ray Brock during their brief marriage. The story of young Mr. Guthrie, along with a friend, on Thanksgiving Day of 1965, getting arrested for dumping the garbage that had accumulated in the church while the Brocks lived there, has become part of America's larger folk cultural narrative. There's scarcely a member of this country's post-World War II generation who doesn't know the story; or who hasn't seen the Arthur Penn movie about the whole incident—some of which was filmed at the site. In the summer of 2009 Arlo appeared on Garrison Keillor's *Prairie Home Companion* when it was being broadcast from Tanglewood, in the Berkshire Mountains of western Massachusetts. When Keillor remarked to Arlo, "You've become quite a celebrity in these parts," Arlo replied, "Well, all I really do is take out the trash." The burst of laughter that immediately arose from the audience was a testament to how much staying power the account of *Alice's Restaurant* has had over the decades.

Thanks to Arlo's initiative and vision the one time home of Alice and Ray Brock is now The Guthrie Center and Interfaith Church Foundation. It sits on Van Deusenville Road close to the Housatonic

River in Great Barrington, Massachusetts. It looks—from the outside—pretty much as it did in 1866 when it was enlarged and renovated to become Trinity Church. It was originally built in 1829 as St. James Chapel. The story now told at many of Arlo Guthrie's concerts, sometimes by his daughter Sarah Lee when she's also taking part, holds that shortly after Arlo acquired the church in the early 1990s he was looking it over and making his plans for it when a local preacher dropped by. The preacher, presumably unaware of whom he was talking to—or of the building's legacy—asked Arlo if he was planning to re-open the place as a church. Arlo replied that indeed he was. When the preacher asked what kind of church—meaning which denomination or faith tradition it would represent—Arlo answered, "Well, it's a 'Bring Your Own God' kind of church."

There's something remarkably appropriate about a "Bring Your Own God" Church serving as a locale that honors the life and legacy of Woody Guthrie. It is a venue for singers—well-known and not so well-known—to perform in a cozy and intimate coffee-house, or cabaret, type of setting. It is also the base of operation for a number of social outreach and social justice programs and initiatives, from local to global. And there are a series of annual benefits held there to support research for a cure for Huntington's Disease, the horribly slow and debilitating malady that took Woody's life in 1967, after some 15 years of his suffering from it.

It's Arlo's place; but it's his father, Woody Guthrie's, place as well. The words to the closing verse of Woody's *Tom Joad*, are clearly displayed as you come through the door:

> *Everybody just might be one big soul,*
> *Well, it looks that way to me.*
> *So wherever you look in the day or the night*
> *That's where I'm going to be.*
> *Wherever folks are fighting for their rights,*
> *That's where I'm going to be, Ma.*
> *That's where I'm going to be.*

Woody took these words as they're spoken by the character of Tom Joad in John Steinbeck's *The Grapes of Wrath*. They certainly stand well enough on their own as lines in Steinbeck's signature novel. But Woody takes them to a more universal level. It was Woody Guthrie's conviction that "everybody just might be one big soul" that gave him the spiritual bond he felt with those whom Jesus termed "the least of these." Woody brought his own God along with him throughout his life; and the idea of God as "one big soul"—with its overtones of Ralph Waldo Emerson's Transcendentalism—was a God who traveled well with him.

Along with Woody's lines from *Tom Joad*, these words from the spiritual teacher Ma Jaya Sati Bhagavati, founder of the Kashi Ashram in Brooklyn, N.Y., are also on display:

> *One God—Many Forms*
> *One River—Many Streams*
> *One People—Many Faces*
> *One Mother—Many Children.*

As related on the Center's website, these words were spoken by this spiritual practitioner and teacher when the Center was first opened and was dedicated to "service to God and (to) all sentient beings." The website narrative goes on to state: "Keeping with the philosophy of Woody and Marjorie Guthrie, for whom these organizations are named, the Guthrie Foundation and Center provide a place where we work on the issues of our time—injecting ourselves into the bloodstream of humanity's best efforts toward a better world."

For a man often "accused" of being a Communist, having his legacy honored in a place with such pronounced religious and spiritual expressions may seem incongruous. But the contention that the work of the Guthrie Center and Interfaith Church is in "keeping with the philosophy of Woody and Marjorie Guthrie" is entirely correct. It is undeniable that Woody Guthrie felt a genuine companionship and comradeship with certain members of the Communist Party in the 1930s and 1940s—the late actor Will

Geer being a case in point; and that he wrote a column for a time for the CP newspaper, *The Daily Worker*; and that he sang at numerous Party sponsored rallies.

But Woody's ultimate motivation for his indefatigable efforts and writings and singing on behalf of struggling working class people was not all that strongly rooted in any kind of hard and fast social or political theory or ideology. Woody just plain didn't do ideology. His final motivation for all of his efforts was a spiritual one, and one that not only drew on the life and teachings of Jesus of Nazareth, but on the wisdom found in many of the world's religious traditions. In his book *Woody, Cisco, and Me: Three in the Merchant Marine*, the author, Jim Lohgi, recounts a conversation in which Woody remarks, "Hell yes, I'm a religious man, but I don't have a favorite, I sorta like them all . . . (and) the ones I admire most in the world are Jesus and Will Rogers." [1] Reflecting on these words, Guthrie scholar Guy Logsdon adds, "To me, he (Guthrie) is saying that life is his church. He knew the Bible well, and one of his favorite books was *The Prophet* by Kahlil Gibran. He was an extremely well read man who knew much about many religions." [2]

Woody's biographers give scant attention to this dimension of his life. They should not be taken to task for this, however. Mr. Guthrie was hardly one to wear his religion on his sleeve. Except for a few songs like *Jesus Christ* or *Christ for President*, very little of Woody's work that got into the public square during his lifetime had any kind of an overtly religious content to it. Maxine "Lefty Lou" Crissman, now in her 96th year (2010), and his KFVD Radio companion from his early Los Angeles days, is quite insistent that Woody was never one to preach religion and never tried to push any kind of religion on anyone. [3] She is, no doubt, absolutely right. Woody even changed the title of his signature song from *God Blessed America for Me* to *This Land Was Made for You and Me* as it began to gain currency. This may have been done to give the song a more secular tone while still preserving its essentially spiritual nature.

During the final and terribly tragic latter stages of his life, however, much of Woody Guthrie's writing took on a definitively religious bent. For as long as he could put pen or pencil to paper—and before the effects of Huntington's Disease prevented even that—Woody wrote voluminously from his hospital settings. In December of 1954, while at Brooklyn State Hospital, he penned a lament in which he alternately expressed his reliance on Jesus: "Jesus Christ, you are my best doctor;" and his longing for death: "I pray every little passing moment to die, die, die." In this same piece of writing he also stated, "All my songs flow out of Christ."(4)

This was not an isolated outburst. At approximately this same time and in this same place, Woody hand wrote a twenty-three page treatise he titled *My Bible*. While the reference is not specifically to the "official" Judeo-Christian Bible, it contains such lines as "My Bible . . . show(s) me just how God is my best healer and God is my best doctor and how it is that Jesus is always my best medicine." (5)

Two years later, after being moved from Brooklyn to the Greystone Park Hospital in New Jersey, Guthrie wrote a play, with its characters based on some of the persons on his ward, which he titled *Forsaken Bibel* (his spelling of Bible in this one). The play is somewhat reminiscent of Ken Kesey's *One Flew Over the Cuckoo's Nest*, but the characters speak in far more religious tones than do Kesey's. At one point the central character, Charley (a variation, presumably, on Woody), takes off on a long soliloquy about his conversations with God. It goes, in part:

> *I do hear you speak to me, god, but no man hears*
> *I do hear you speak new to me in no man's language*
> *I do hear you, god, talkin' to me in words no human knows*
> *In no known lingo, in no worldly tone*
> *I do hear you, god, sing to me above all man's miseries*(6)

Could all this be Woody's own version of "fox hole religion"? That is to say, the desperate clutching of a dying man in the midst of excruciatingly prolonged suffering? At first take it might appear that way. But if seen from the perspective of the larger context of his life and writings, much of what came from Woody's pen in his final years actually draws upon, and is reflective of, personal and spiritual wellsprings that had been there all along. To be sure, his personal life was marked by numerous flaws and failures that our wildly imperfect humanity leaves us vulnerable to. But to say that his life was marked by certain personal flaws and serious shortcomings is a far cry from saying it was ultimately defined by them. What ultimately defined Woody Guthrie's life was an intense spiritual bond he felt not only with his fellow human beings, but with all of Being Itself. When he wrote, then, "All of my songs flow out of Christ" he was actually referring, I believe, to this greater, Universal Connection he felt with All of Life. Because Christianity was the particular religion with which he was most familiar, he writes, in this passage anyway, of his Universal Connection using Christian language.

At the same time, however, in the songs and writings that are reflective of his spirituality Woody hardly confined himself to Christian language and thought. Recalling Guy Logsdon's observations, Guthrie was a true Universalist when it came to expressing his religious and spiritual inclinations. Much of what he wrote in this genre has only come to light in more recent years, long after his death, and has been set to music and recorded by other artists. Songs like *Holy Ground, This Morning I Am Born Again, God's Promise,* and *Heaven*—to name but a few—never even became songs for Woody. They were among the hundreds of verses he wrote as inspiration led him. As just noted, they've been set to music and recorded by others like Ellis Paul, or Slaid Cleaves, or The Klezmatics. But the lyrics themselves point to the passion that ultimately drove Woody Guthrie's life and work.

Much of what has been touched on here will be revisited in greater detail in the chapters ahead. Woody was not raised with a structured and deliberate kind of religious education, in the manner, say, of Jack Kerouac's Catholicism. His sister, Mary Jo Guthrie Edgmon, points out: "If you read his book *Bound for Glory,* I believe from his writings (one can see) it would have been impossible for (Woody to have had) any kind of a structured, supervised routine for any kind of religion." But then, writing of herself and her siblings as they were all being raised, she continues, "It was in our hearts to do good. The Ten Commandments were our guidelines. We were taught love and kindness for each other, honesty always, honor for our parents, faith, good morals. We were ruled by Jesus and said the Lord's Prayer regularly. These rules were set forth by our father, Charley, and were imbedded in us forever." (7) In the pages ahead it is my hope to offer a deeper look into what it was that was "embedded" in Woody Guthrie forever.

In the end there's really no need for a Church of Woody Guthrie. The "congregation" of those persons around the world—past, present, and future—who have been touched and blessed by his life and work are "church" enough. But that small structure sitting there next to the Housatonic River in western Massachusetts—a locale Woody himself never even laid eyes on—is as good a tribute to his life as one will find out there.

> *One God—Many Forms*
> *One River—Many Streams*
> *One People—Many Faces*
> *One Mother—Many Children.*

Surely, Woody Guthrie could say "Amen!" to that.

CHAPTER TWO

Strong in the Broken Places: Okemah and Pampa

For anyone taking a close and in-depth look at the life of Woody Guthrie, the question would have to arise: What kept him from being a broken and cynical man by the time he reached the cusp of adulthood? While he was born into a stable and reasonably financially secure family, the hardships and the back and forth pendulum swings his family experienced in Woody's early years, and on through to his late adolescence, could have tainted him for life. If anyone could have made a case for life being a stacked deck against him, with no discernable way out, it could well have been Woody Guthrie by the time he reached the age of twenty.

Then, in his later years and a few years before the effects of Huntington's chorea began taking their toll on him, Woody and his second wife, Marjorie, experienced the loss of their four year old daughter, Cathy, in an apartment fire in Brooklyn, New York. Woody had a very special love for this child of his—whom he called "Stackabones"—and such a devastating loss could have ruined what life he had left at that point.

8

In each of these cases however, from his early and then latter years, Woody Guthrie found the internal resources to prevail over the trials and tragedies that befell him rather than being overcome by them. What kinds of spiritual wellsprings was he drawing on? The following two chapters will explore that question.

His earliest years in Okemah, Oklahoma, as both Woody and his biographers tell it, were safe and secure and even promising. At the time of the birth of his third child in 1912, Charley Guthrie had a successful real estate business going in Okemah, both selling and renting out properties, and was seen as a "comer" in the Democratic Party of that time and place. The family, consisting of Charley and his wife Nora, and an older brother and sister of Woody's (Roy and Clara), lived in a six room house. This is how Woody recalls it in *Bound for Glory:*

"(In those) days our family seemed to be getting along all right. People rode down our street in buggies and sarries all dressed up, and they'd look over at our house and say, 'Charlie and Nora Guthrie's place. Right new.' . . . Papa went to town and made real estate deals with other people, and he brought their money home. Mama could sign a check for any amount, buy every little thing her eyes liked the looks of. Roy and Clara could stop off in any store in Okemah, and buy new clothes to fit the weather, new things to eat to make you healthy, and Papa was proud because we could have anything we saw. Our house was packed full of things Mama liked, Roy liked, Clara liked, and that was what Papa liked. I remember his leather law books, Blackstone and others . . . I guess I was going on three then."[1]

In a town like Okemah in the years leading up to World War I that was probably about as good as it could get. For the Guthries, however, it was not to last. Woody may have been overplaying it a bit in the above passage as a way of setting up the heights reached before the fall that later came. But whatever the heights may have been, the fall did come in a series of events in the years that unfolded after his "going on three."

Before Woody reached the age of five his mother, Nora, was already beginning to show signs of seeming mental instability—

signs that would never be correctly diagnosed as the onset of Huntington's Disease. She could go from singing songs with Woody and his siblings at the piano in their home to dragging the furniture in the home out into the front yard. She could he loving and nurturing at one moment, and distant and distracted and even angry the next. In the midst of these mood swings Nora gave birth to her and Charley's fourth child, George, in 1918. Woody's two older siblings were Clara and Roy.

Then there were the fires. An oil burner fire partially destroyed the house the Guthries were living in in the fall of 1916 when Woody was four. They were able to recover from that fire incident well enough, but not the one that came nearly three years later in May of 1919. Precisely how it happened is open to question, but Clara Guthrie set her dress on fire with the kerosene oil used for cooking and heating. Initially it looked like she might recover, but she died from the effects of the wounds soon thereafter. According to his biographer Ed Cray, the last time Woody Guthrie cried was at Clara's funeral. He was seven years old.

Things did not get much better for the Guthries in the years that followed. Even as her condition worsened, Nora gave birth to a fifth child, Mary Jo, in 1922. By now the family fortunes that Woody described in *Bound for Glory* had taken a serious downturn in the boom and bust years in the Oklahoma oil fields. In an attempt at a fresh start the family briefly moved to Oklahoma City; but whatever plans Charley had didn't pan out and they returned to Okemah only a year later. Woody's description of the Guthrie's return to his hometown stands in marked contrast to his recounting of their earlier years there:

"I was standing up in the truck with my feet on our old sofa waving both hands in the air when we hit the city limits of Okemah . . . . I looked a mile away and saw the old slaughter pen where the wild dogs had chased me across the cut stubble. I looked to the south and seen the vacant lots I'd fought in a million times. My eyes knew everything at a glance.

"When the old truck crawled past Ninth Street, Roy stuck his head out on his side of the cab and yelled, 'See anything you know, Woodsaw?"

"'Yeah!' I guess I sounded pretty washed out. 'Home where Clara burned up.'

"I spotted a couple of kids jumping across a plowed hill. 'Hi! Matt! Nick! I'm back! See? All of us!'

"'Hi! Come play with us!' 'Where ya livin'?' They waved back at me.

"'Old Jim Cain house! East end!'"

Then Woody goes on: "They ducked their heads and didn't ask me to come and play with them anymore."(2)

From the decrepit "Jim Cain house" in the less desirable section of Okemah, things continued to go even further downhill. Over the course of the ensuing three years Charley Guthrie was injured in a fire and his health declined. Then Charley, George, and Mary Jo moved to Pampa, Texas to live with one of Charley's sisters. As Nora's condition continued to deteriorate she was sent to the state mental hospital in Norman, Oklahoma. She would later die there in June of 1930. At the age of 15 Woody was more or less on his own on the streets of Okemah, before being taken in by a family named Moore. When the Moores moved away Woody found himself living in a tin shack in Okemah while attending the local high school. Soon thereafter, in 1929, and shortly before the Stock Market crashed, Woody also moved to Pampa to help his father Charley with a job he'd be able to land managing a boarding house.

In today's parlance seventeen year old Woody Guthrie would have been labeled an "at risk" youth, as he scrambled for whatever kind of a life he could find for himself on the streets of Pampa. He made a try at resuming his high school studies but never managed to graduate. Instead he drifted between working with his father at the boarding house to whatever other nickel and dime jobs he could pick up around town. He was on the kind of life track that could well have had him in jail or dead before getting out of his twenties. Such was the fate of many other young men of his time and circumstance.

But something else happened instead. Somewhere within the person of Woody Guthrie came a moment—or more—of self-reflection. He describes the moment in *Bound for Glory*: "I wanted to . . . be on my own hook. I walked the streets in the drift of the dust, and wondered where I was bound for, where I was going, what I was going to do. My whole life turned into one big question mark. And I was the only living person who could answer it."(3)

There's something quite remarkable in these very plain spoken, and plainly written words. As precarious, uncertain, and "at risk" as his life was at that time—and not even being out of his teens—Woody, as this passage demonstrates, felt he had the internal resources to deal with the "one big question mark" he took his life to be. However much outside circumstances—very cruel circumstances more often than not—had dictated and determined his life to that point, young Woody was determined not to be defined by them, much less blame them for his fate. He is describing a spiritual moment in the words cited above; a spiritual moment, in this case, being a time when one is driven to both look inside and beyond the self in seeking answers—partial and incomplete as they may be—to ultimate questions. He is describing here the beginning of his life-long search for some greater meaning, some greater purpose, to his existence. In the last analysis this is a religious search and journey.

According to the theologian Michael Novak two fundamental religious questions are "Who am I?" and then "Who are we, under these stars?" To put it more broadly, these questions have to do with how we grasp and understand our essential humanity; and how we grasp and understand our relationship to all that is beyond the self, i.e. "we, under these stars." While he may not have used Novak's (or my) language, there was something within the soul of Woody Guthrie that brought him to an encounter with these questions of existence, even as he was barely scraping by when it came to attending to his baseline physical existence.

Woody was hardly in a position at this point in his life to set forth on some kind of a spiritual pilgrimage to a distant holy land. He had to keep his pilgrimage within the confines of 1930s Pampa,

Texas, and find whatever greater meaning for his life as he could in that locale. So he took his search to the Pampa library. To pick up his story again: "I went to the town library and scratched around in the books. I carried them home by the dozens and by the armloads, on any subject. I didn't care which. I wanted to look into everything a little bit, and pick out something, *something that would turn me into a human being of some kind* (emphasis added).(4)

"Something that would turn me into a human being of some kind . . ." Even as he still had to scratch out a living for himself, Woody Guthrie was also searching for his humanity. A local Pampa historian, Thelma Bray, describes the landscape of Woody Guthrie's journey of discovery, of his quest for "something that would turn me into a human being of some kind:"

"New schools and new churches were being built. Woodrow Wilson School was built on the east side of town . . . Churches were built in all parts of town by the Methodists, Baptists, Catholics, Presbyterians, Free Christians, Episcopalians, and Church of Christ . . . From 1929 to 1931 the 'Million Dollar Row' was built consisting of the four story Schneider Hotel, the Central Fire Station, the City Hall, the Gray Country Courthouse and the Combs Worley Building.

"Pampa was also becoming a cultural center, providing a city library, musical concerts, and opportunities for musicians to perform. Woody spent many hours in the city library devouring every available book, including books on philosophy, psychology, and religion.

"During those years, much of the country was suffering a depression after the Wall Street crash in 1929. But the Depression did not hit Pampa when the rest of the country was suffering because of the oil boom in the area and the basic prosperity."(5)

Pampa, Texas, then, provided Woody Guthrie an oasis of a sort—an intellectual and cultural oasis in the midst of the Depression—where he could begin to cultivate a life of the mind and spirit. To pick up Ms. Bray's account again: "Music was an important part of Woody's life in Pampa, but so were the many times he went to the library . . . As can be noted in Woody's own words, he had a drive, a determination, to make something of himself during those years he was living in Pampa."(6)

Guthrie biographer Ed Cray echoes Thelma Bray's recollections: "Guthrie systematically worked his way through the (library) shelves, concentrating on psychology, Western religion, Eastern philosophies, what (brother-in-law to be Matt) Jennings called 'yogi stuff.' Guthrie read the newly published mystical parables of Lebanese-American poet Kahlil Gibran *The Prophet*. 'He just wanted to know something about everything in the world.' Matt explained."(7)

Woody lived in Pampa from 1929 until the spring of 1937 when he departed for California. Those eight years were especially formative for him. With his high school friend, Matt Jennings, he developed an interest in music and found an affinity for playing, singing, and composing songs. In 1931 he and Matt and another local aspiring musician named Cluster Baker formed the Corn Cob trio and got some local gigs. Woody kept bouncing around from job to job, attending but never finishing high school. In October of 1933 Woody married Matt's younger sister, Mary. He was 21 and she was 16 years old. His father, Charley, also got remarried at about the same time to a woman named Bettie Jean. The first of the three children he would have with Mary was born in October of 1935.

All the while Woody kept up his religious explorations. His step-mother, Bettie Jean, presented herself to the citizenry of Pampa as a faith healer and fortune teller. She even managed to make something of a living from it and her step-son, Woody, was intrigued with her trade for a time. Woody also briefly came under the influence of a charismatic Church of Christ preacher, the Reverend E.C. McKenzie. So strong was Rev. McKenzie's impact on Woody that he had himself baptized into the Church of Christ. But like most of his explorations, this just proved to be one more stop on Woody's spiritual road.

It was in that same year of 1935 that the first major dust storm hit Pampa. To whatever extent the town may have been spared the harsher effects of the Depression up to that point, the ravaging of the land caused Woody to conclude—as did many others of that time and place—that he would have to seek a living elsewhere. In March of 1937, with his and Mary's second child on the way, Woody—now a 25 year old young man—headed west for California.

He left behind him the rise and fall of the family fortunes in Okemah, as well as his up and down hardscrabble years in Pampa. But what he took with him was the genesis of a philosophy of life, engendered by his desire to "turn (himself) into a human being of some kind." Just as Woody was leaving Pampa his brother Roy and his wife Ann saw the birth of their first child, a girl named Mary Ann. On February 5, 1937, some five months shy of his twenty-fifth birthday, Woody Guthrie wrote a letter to his newborn niece imparting to her whatever wisdom he had gained to that point. In some respects the letter serves as a summation of what Woody had gleaned from the books in the Pampa library along with the other personal explorations he'd made to that point. These are some of its more select passages:

"Let me be the first to congratulate you and greet you upon your entrance into this world. You will find it an odd place to spend a few years . . . Let you faith in Providence remain careless, desireless, and firm . . . and fear nothing. Love and trust all and no harm shall appear on the horizon of your noonday. A mind of fear creates twisted lives and brings about the very conditions feared. Evil is unreal. Fear nothing . . . Love for love's sake. For God is love. Hate nobody. Harm no living thing. Live to help and serve always.

"Think. Do your own of this. If somebody else were supposed to do it for you another head would be on your shoulders. Your head is your own for a reason. Think upon it till you find it. Then use it thus.

"Concentrate long and deep upon your life and living—death and dying—who, what, why are we as we are and where are we going. The answer, your answer, will at a time come in all plainness. Then you will know. More valuable this than schooling. More wiser than ruling, No fooling!

"Life is a proposition of giving. Give and live. Crave and die . . ." (8)

When he gets to the eighth and ninth pages of this nine page handwritten letter, Woody's words become something of a prayer. While not addressed to a deity, he is addressing his prayer both to his newborn niece as well as to whatever he senses may be beyond them both:

"May your days be toward a glittering harvest when your seasons blend at noontide and your morning stoops to kiss your midday. May your gladness ripen as a yellow sweetfruit and the radiance of your thinking invigorate the world. May you forget yourself serving others as the raindrops dash themselves to pieces to cool the dusty earth. May you see the non-reality of affliction and realize the allness of God. For God is truth, love. May you never include the word enemy in your vocabulary. *May you express your innermost self nobly. May you glance into the world religions and philosophies and form a conception of the true worth and value as a highest standard, a worthy purpose.* (Emphasis added) . . . May you pass beyond the seventh veil and solve the riddle of human life and destiny. May your good deeds lead you to the highest physical (and) mental, development and mastery possible. May you attain."

He then signs it: "With love always, W. Guthrie—The Soul Doctor."(9)

The Soul Doctor. Was this the image that twenty-five year old Woody Guthrie had cultivated for himself at this point in his life? Without, I hope, getting too psychological about it I feel this letter can be read as a credo Woody addresses to himself, with his niece being the channel through which he brings his desires and yearnings back to himself. Yes, the words are—quite sincerely, I feel—meant for his niece. But on some deeper level Woody is also reaching out to himself for some spiritual grounding as he leaves his dual places of origin, and moves into the next phase of his life. He is the soul doctor—tending to the needs of his own soul as much as those of any other.

The ten years that followed Woody Guthrie's departure from Pampa, and which are touched upon in other chapters, proved to be his peak years in terms of his creativity, productivity, activism, and widespread recognition. And it was ten years after his departing Pampa that Woody Guthrie again was faced with the need to draw upon some of the deepest wellsprings of spiritual sustenance he possessed when he encountered what surely must have been the greatest tragedy of his life.

CHAPTER THREE

Strong in the Broken Places:
Losing Stackabones

In February of 1947 Woody Guthrie was living in Brooklyn, New York with his second wife, Marjorie Greenblatt Guthrie. A rambling man for most of his life, New York had now become his base of operation. Only ten years had gone by since Woody had departed Pampa, Texas for California, but they were truly event-full years. He had gained a wide circle of friends in a variety of arenas: Through his involvement in the labor movement with persons like actor Will Geer, with activist musicians like Pete Seeger and Lee Hays, and through his stint in the United States Merchant Marine during World War II. In the ten years from 1937 to 1947 the name "Woody Guthrie" had become known "from California to the New York Island," as his best known song—which he'd written in 1940—put it.

To whatever extent he may have found at least some answers to the "one big question mark" of his life that he'd encountered back in Pampa, and to whatever extent he'd discovered what it meant to be a human being of some kind, and to whatever extent he'd solved the "riddle of human destiny," as he put it in that 1937 letter to his new-born niece, Woody Guthrie remained as vulnerable as any human being to some of life's inexplicable tragedies. On the afternoon of February 9, 1947 an electrical fire broke out in Woody's and Marjorie's Brooklyn apartment, and ignited the mattress where their four year old daughter, Cathy, was taking a nap. Marjorie had briefly stepped out to run an errand and Woody was away for the day. In a way hauntingly reminiscent of Clara Guthrie in the aftermath of her being burned back in Okemah nearly 30 years earlier, Cathy, at the hospital to which she was taken, talked about burning her dress and about her nursery school friends and teachers. The following morning of February 10 she slipped into a coma and died.

While he no doubt loved and cared about all of his children, Woody's devotion to Cathy was in a category all of its own. He nicknamed her "Stackabones." She was a major source of inspiration for a number of the children's songs he wrote and recorded. In *Woody, Cisco, and Me* Jim Longhi describes Woody's reaction as the Merchant Marine ship they were on returned to New York after a seafaring run: "When we were in sight of Coney Island Woody waved and shouted, 'I'm a comin' Momma Marjorie. I'm a comin' Missie Stackabones!'"(1)

In the days following Cathy's death letters and telegrams of condolences poured in from family members, close friends, as well as from complete strangers who, while they had never even met Woody Guthrie, felt a connection with him nonetheless. Some 35-40 of these letters, and Woody's replies to them, are preserved in the Guthrie Archives. To read them is to be both tremendously moved, and to gain special insight into Woody's sources of inner strength and spirituality. Woody answered practically every letter he and Marjorie received. Most of his replies were typewritten, single spaced, and filled up a full page. In a letter to Lee Hays Woody states his desire to respond to all of those from whom he hears: "Your telegram is here on the table while I write . . . your words made us feel lots better . . . We are answering all the wires and letters as we come to them here in the pile." (2)

In some of the letters he writes Woody recounts, at some length, the details of Cathy's terrible fate. While some persons in such a situation might choose to shy away from, or not want to face at all, a recounting of such a devastating event, Woody seems to need to tell it several times over. It's as if he's trying to exorcize the experience of his loss—to get it outside of himself while also not denying its reality and finality.

He also appears to struggle at times with the various explanations that are offered him and Marjorie for Cathy's death. In the wake of such a tragedy the first impulse of family, friends, and even strangers alike is to try to offer some words of comfort. While the impulse is completely understandable and even commendable, such words can sometimes create as much conflict as they can provide comfort; conflict in the sense of creating conflicted feelings in the ones for whom the words of comfort are intended. Woody appears to appreciate all the intended words of comfort that are offered, while also feeling conflicted about them as he and Marjorie deal with their loss. In a letter to a Marcia Copel he writes:

"Lots of folks have told us the old story about the child who was born in such a dark world, too bright a light to shine here and so had to be taken by high powers to shine elsewhere . . . Others told us she came to do her job of making us love one another, to draw together friends and enemies, and doing this in her years took her off to glory . . . Others say she loved too many people and the Lord took her to teach the rest of us a hard lesson or two of the hard kind. We hear everything." But then he goes on to add, "We do not believe any of these things even when said by fervent lips of some true believer . . ." (3)

But later, in other letters, he softens this stance to the point of appearing to reverse himself. In a letter to Maria Smith we find these words: "We heard people say everything about her. We heard all of their faiths and their beliefs and their religions, their philosophies and idle thoughts. We believed them all and loved them all and took them all in, the same as we loved and admired your nice card of sympathy and new faith.' (4)

Woody goes, then, from "We do not believe any of these things" to "We believe them all." What's really going on here has to do with the human ability and the human need, on the part of those who have experienced an overwhelming loss, to be receptive to whatever comfort is offered. In the grieving process, particularly in the close aftermath of the loss, there are indeed times when nothing helps and when anything that is offered actually seems like a mockery. This usually occurs when anger and bewilderment, again quite understandably, get the upper hand for a time. But then there are other times when the anger and bewilderment subside and the heart opens up and takes in whatever expressions of comfort and healing are offered regardless of whatever words are used. And no one has any control over what mode of grief comes into play when. What we witness in these two letters, I feel, is Woody's movement between these two modes of grief.

Woody himself did realize and understand the difficulty in writing the kinds of letters he and Marjorie were receiving. He acknowledged as much in a letter to Lou Kleinman: "Your letter was one of the first to come to us, giving us the kind of strength we all need to face this thing in the way that Cathy would have liked. Nobody can write a very good letter when the letter is about death and dying. Nobody . . . can make it any better. But words such as yours sure did help us in taking up a new hold and starting out all over again." (5)

So, as conflicted as he may have been at times with all the condolences he and his wife received, for the most part Woody does maintain a stance of gratitude and receptivity to all that is offered them, whether he accepts the belief stance reflected in the words or not. Here's what he got from his now 68 year old father, Charley, who as we have already seen, certainly bore his share of loss and grief in his life: "We all know that God in His Infinite Wisdom knows best and acts best in all things. And though we mourn her passing,

Her star has gone down
To rise upon a fairer shore
There, bright as Heaven's jeweled crown

To shine forever more." (6)

It is doubtful that Woody's spirituality, at this point in his life, could have accommodated such sentiments as these—not in any literal sense anyway. And yet perhaps these words from his father recalled for Woody the faith to which he was first exposed in his earliest years in Okemah, and offered him some comfort in that regard. There is no record available of any response Woody made to his father, but in a note to his brother, George, he did say, "I never did see two people as spiritually close together as Marjorie and Cathy, as Cathy and Marjorie." (7) He did see, then, his and Marjorie's relationship to their daughter in spiritual terms.

At this point in his life Woody had developed a spiritual, if not mystical, attachment to what he most generally referred to as "the people." He meant, most likely, people who were continually having to struggle to make a living and to make something of their lives beyond the sheer rubrics of existence. To whatever extent he may have romanticized the working class, the image he held of "the people" did give Woody Guthrie a sense of commitment and attachment to an entity and a power greater than himself. This spiritual attachment, to be sure, was grounded in Woody's very down to earth dealings with working folks and the desperate circumstances in which many of them often found themselves. In some of the letters he wrote following Cathy's death he invokes this attachment and ties it in to his feelings for his deceased daughter. In one to a fellow he only refers to as "Slim" we find this:

"Well, you can see, Slim, just how crazy and unexplainable all this is, and that is the hard part. A thing such as this, if we let it, will eat and burn into both of us, Marjorie and myself, and wreck our whole lives . . . We have decided not to drain away the last drops of our lives by beating our gums about this twisted affair . . . Your letter, Slim, did make us lift up our faces another inch towards the open sky." (8)

Woody's way of not allowing his and Marjorie's loss to completely eat and burn into them is to lift his eyes up to "the people," as his letter goes on to indicate: "The worse thing that can happen to you is to cut yourself loose from people. And the best thing is to sort of vaccinate yourself right into the big stream and blood of the people; to feel like you know the best and worst of folks, that you see everywhere and never feel weak or lost or lonesome anywhere. There is just one thing that can cut you to drifting from the people and that is any brand or style of greed. There is just one way to save yourself and that is to get together and work and fight for everybody." (9) As he reaches beyond himself for some greater purpose and greater meaning in the face of his and his wife's horrible loss, Woody's impulse is to inject (vaccinate) himself into "the big stream . . . of the people." This, again, is not an unusual way of coping with an overwhelming tragedy, which is to seek some spiritual relief by dedicating—or in Woody's case—by re-dedicating oneself to some greater good that will in some way give some meaning to the tragedy itself.

This same theme carries through in a letter he writes to Pete Seeger and to Pete's family: "Lots of letters piled here from Cathy's nursery school teachers. They say that Cathy was the only child they had ever seen who was completely happy in every way. Lots of friends, relations, told us this same thing. So there is little sorrow left in Cathy's tracks to think about or write to you about. Her four years were wild and full. She was a full seasoned citizen around here . . . She put the neighborhood several generations ahead of itself, woke up many friends, and set many folks to loving one another that used to be hard enemies." (10)

Woody then urges Pete to encourage Cathy's qualities in his (Pete's) son, Danny: "Give your little Danny this same kind of progressive love and a voice around your place there. Give him your careers to run and your friends to make . . . Give him your crazy feelings, your ups and downs, give him everything . . . (and) he will give you wild and dancy limbs and leaves, the closest and truest contact and closeness, your own mental rights to operate and to live and to work in your highest shapes and forms . . . Be like Danny and he will be a bit like you. I guess I could call this letter my letter from Stackabones to Danny." (11)

Woody is attempting to give daughter Cathy a kind of immortality here. He sees in his deceased daughter some of the same values and principles and ideals that he, Woody, was also seeking to embody. He then urges his best friend to cultivate these same qualities in his son: "Let him (Danny) in as a little grown up, for he will be the most grown up amongst you." (12) This is what Woody wanted from, and even saw in, his daughter—a little grown up who would be the most grown up amongst him and his friends.

Then, as Woody concludes his letter to Pete, he picks up his theme of "the people" as he sees in Cathy a guiding light to continue in his own pursuit of his vision: "This (all I've written) all comes from the people Marjorie loves, from the people I know and love, from the fine progressive and revolutionary thinkers that met and gave to Cathy her love for the ugliest person on the street. She had the real spirit of a Peoples Dancer and of a Peoples Singer and if I ever display any sign of either spirit it will be because of what Cathy taught me with great patience and pains during her trip through here." (13)

It would be easy enough to see this letter to Pete Seeger as Woody projecting his own needs and desires and aspirations onto his deceased four-year-old daughter, and turning her into an iconic "Saint Cathy." Such often happens in the home where a young child dies. He or she becomes beatified by the family as a way of coping with their grief over the loss. But such psychologizing, for whatever kernels of truth it may contain, does not do justice to the full range of thoughts and feelings Woody Guthrie expresses here. Granted, he is looking and reaching for ways of dealing with Cathy's death. But in the very act of reaching he is also finding a re-commitment to the deepest ideals and visions to which he'd devoted his life. Out of this horrible loss does come a renewed spirituality on Woody Guthrie's part.

One of the better insights into Woody's overall religious and spiritual stance at this point in his life is found in a reply to a letter he received from a woman that neither he nor Marjorie even knew. Her name was Effie Holladay and she had some apparent ties to Texas and Oklahoma from around the same time Woody was living there. She closes her letter by writing, "May the Divine

Activity of the Christ Mind transform and prosper your life and fulfill all your needs." (14)

In responding to this stranger, Woody says, "I liked your sentence about teaching people to bear up under their own sorrows and their own troubles. You sound to me like a true believer in Christ Science or Scientific Christianity or a Christian Scientist . . . Anyway, no matter what your faith may be, Jewish, Catholic, Protestant, Atheist, Christian Scientist, Buddhist, Mohammedan, or any of the handful of others, I want to tell you (you can) get your helpful and instructive thoughts, ideas, visions, and hopes (from them)." (15)

Woody then goes on to personalize what he's just said: "I myself am a master and a student of all faiths and all creeds, seeing the same general spiritual feelings and ideas present in them all—that as always living in the oneness of the human race, its blending and its mixtures of all colors, all kinds. I thank you again for thinking of me and my wife . . ." (16) The gist of these words later found expression in a song Woody would write, but never set to music, called *God's Promise:* "I give you my peace and my strength to pull home, My love for my races all creeds and all kinds . . . My love for my saviors, all colors all kinds . . ."

"I myself am a master and a student of all faiths and all creeds . . . always living in the oneness of the human race." This can well be seen as an updated expression of what is found in the letter he'd composed to his new born niece ten years earlier in which he signed off as "The Soul Doctor." And it was Woody's identification with the "oneness of the human race" that helped sustain him in what was quite likely the most trying time of his life. As he worked his way through his responses to the expressions of condolences he and Marjorie received, Woody Guthrie became his own Soul Doctor.

CHAPTER FOUR

Woody and Jesus

In the summer of 1941 while spending time in Portland, Oregon writing songs for the Bonneville Power Authority, the best known of which would be "Roll On Columbia," Woody wrote a letter to Pete Seeger, Millard Lampell, and Lee Hays about his experiences with some of the farm workers there. By now his reputation was such that the name Woody Guthrie had some substantial currency to it. A portion of Woody's letter reads as follows:

"I have visited the Okie camps a time or two since I've been out here and they put me on their programs and the crowds were almost too big for you to believe . . . And I made it my business to go to a lot of the tents and shacks this trip that I didn't make on the other trips, and hear them all sing, the little sisters, brothers, yodelers, ma and pa in the old yaller light of a coal oil lamp . . . And I make a little speech in each tent and I said, 'You folks are the best in the West. Why don't you take some time out and write up some songs about who you are, where you come from, what you was a lookin for, and the things you want to do.'

"Every one of them would lean and look towards me and keep so still and such a solemn look on their faces, there in those little old greasy hovels that would bring the rising sun to tears. In a few minutes some young and dreaming member of the family would break down and say, I been a thinkin about that ever since I commenced a singin. And then the whole bunch would enter into a deeper religious conversation and decide that was right. On more than one night, on more than one day, I've heard my Okie friends ask me, 'Say Mister, you don't happen to be Mister Jesus do you? Come back?'" (1)

It would have been easy enough for Woody Guthrie to have shrugged off, or laughed off, the idea that he was the Second Coming of Jesus Christ; and while there's no evidence at all that he ever saw himself as such, it is clear from the overall tone of this letter that the experiences he describes in it affected him deeply. The question "You don't happen to be Mister Jesus, do you?" touched Woody enough for him mention it in a letter to three of his close friends. Guthrie had a mystical connection with the dispossessed persons of his day; so much so that some of them, as this letter indicates, actually connected him with the accounts of the life of Jesus.

Jesus lived his life with, and took his teachings to, the down and outers of first century Palestine; even as Woody Guthrie did the same with the throw-aways of his time and place. One can only speculate what might have been in Woody's mind and heart as he walked away from a gathering of his fellow "Okies" who, in their desperate circumstances, had earnestly asked him if he were "Mister Jesus."

The timing of this letter evokes a certain parallel between the life of Woody Guthrie and a story from the Jesus Narratives of the Christian Gospels. Several months prior to the summer of 1941 Woody had deliberately turned his back on commercial success. CBS Radio in New York City put him on the air with a show called *Pipe Smoking Time*, sponsored by Model Tobacco. He was to open each show with a singing commercial that went, in part:

> Load up your pipe and take your life easy
> With Model Tobacco to light up your way
> We're glad to be with you today.

The gig paid Woody $180.00 a week; about $2500.00 a week in 2010 dollars. Practically swimming in money, he sent for his first wife, Mary Jennings Guthrie, and their three children to come to New York from Pampa, Texas. He'd come a long way from scrounging on the streets of Okemah and Pampa. But Woody apparently was unable to live on Easy Street for very long. On the first week of January of 1941 he told Mary that they and the kids were leaving New York City and hitting the road again—going back to the Los Angeles area to try to reconnect with old friends there. The *Pipe Smoking Time* people wanted to package Woody as an authentic country-style American everyman. But "packaged authenticity" didn't quite work for Woody Guthrie. In addition, he was not willing to be, in effect, a prop to sell a product. He was out the door barely before he made it in.

The Gospel accounts of Matthew and Luke tell of the temptation of Jesus by the Devil following his baptism. One of these temptations has Satan showing Jesus the "kingdoms of the world" and telling Jesus all of it can be his if he, Jesus, will worship him. In effect Jesus is offered the wealth of the world if he will give his soul over to the Devil. Jesus' response is "Get thee behind me, Satan" (Matthew 4, verse 10).

Woody may not have felt like he was being asked to sell his soul to the Devil; but apparently he did feel that he was being asked to sell out his principles for the sake of worldly success. This is the content, as Woody told it, of his resignation letter to Model Tobacco: "Dear Sirs, I have smoked your tobacco. I've chewed your tobacco, and I've even snuffed your tobacco. But I'll be goddamned if I'll have your tobacco shoved up my ass." (2) That may not exactly be "Get thee behind me Satan," but the sentiment is similar.

These two stories of Woody Guthrie and Jesus Christ, different as they are in content and style, both involve an individual refusing success and power—as defined by the conventional standards of his day—for the sake of a higher good and calling. Jesus walked away from worldly temptation to live a life in which he tried to bring some measure of hope and kindness and justice to the outcasts of his day. A few months after walking away what would have been—in early 21st century dollars—an annual salary of over $130,000 Woody finds himself "in little greasy hovels that would being the rising sun to tears," trying to give the inhabitants of these hovels some measure of hope and dignity.

(For the sake of honesty, however, it should be noted that Jesus, so far as we know, wasn't dragging a wife and three very young kids around with him; and making their lives extremely difficult, for the sake of a "higher calling." This issue will be taken up in a later chapter titled "The Holy Paradox.")

While Woody most likely did not regard himself as "Mister Jesus," he nonetheless felt a strong sense of identity with the man, Jesus of Nazareth. He, Guthrie, had no apparent use for all of the theological wranglings that arose after Jesus' earthly ministry—and which continue to this day—about to who he was, or whether or not he was also God, or the Son of God, or the Second Person of the Trinity, or any other such esoteric speculations. It was not the finer points of theology, vis a vis the person of Jesus, that interested Woody in the least. In a sense Woody projected his vision and passion of a free, fair, and just world for the working people of the world onto the image of Jesus as contained in the New Testament Gospels.

It would be more accurate, however, to say that Woody projected his vision onto *an* image of Jesus. The greatest irony, when it comes to the person of Jesus, is that the man who has perhaps the greatest name recognition in the Western world, is the same person about whom very little is actually known. The New Testament Gospels are not biographies of Jesus of Nazareth, in the sense that biography is understood today. They are more like religious tracts produced by the First and Second Century Church, purporting to "prove" a conclusion about Jesus that the Church was seeking to propagate—namely that he was the one and only begotten Son of God. Just who the actual, and highly mysterious, Jesus-person was who lay behind the Early Church's theological overlay of him is virtually impossible to determine.

The result of this mystery is that the person of Jesus—whoever he was—is akin to a Rorschach blot upon which all manner of speculation and interpretation can be projected. Granted, to be sure, the Gospel accounts of the life of Jesus are considerably more defined than an ink blot on a page, in that they do tell a discernable story. But—and this is where the Rorschach analogy holds—the Jesus Narrative itself is still vague enough, and open-ended enough, to invite, as noted, a wide range of interpretation and projection. Most human projections, as any psychologist will attest, come from a human need or desire to see, and take, what we need or desire from a particular object, individual, story, picture, etc. In the person of Jesus of Nazareth, as portrayed in the New Testament Gospels, Woody Guthrie found his archetype working class/working people's hero.

To say this is a projection, as is being suggested here however, is in no way meant to dismiss or denigrate Woody's take on Jesus. However much his folksy ways and mannerisms and language may have disguised it, Woody Guthrie was a scholar—probably one of the most unpretentious scholars to ever live, but a scholar nonetheless. And one of the many areas in which he had a good store of knowledge and wisdom was religion (along with politics, literature, art, and music to name a few other areas). He knew what the Christian Gospels had to say, and he may have had some familiarity with the emerging field of Biblical scholarship and critique that began to develop in the mid-to-late 19th century. As he worked his way through the store of books in the Pampa, Texas library it is a good possibility that he came across some reasonably learned Biblical commentary. Even if this cannot be directly substantiated, it is still a reasonable assumption. As was pointed out in a previous chapter Woody's introduction to the Pampa library came from the wife of the minister of the First Christian Church of Pampa. So Woody Guthrie's projection of a need and desire for a working class hero was not a fabrication, but rather what he extracted from his knowledge of the Jesus Story and his understanding of how it came to be told.

As stated in the opening chapter, Woody did not have a formal religious education in the sense of going to Church and Sunday School on a regular basis while he was growing up. As his sister,

Mary Jo, notes, "We didn't get up on Sunday morning and get dressed and go to church." But there was still an identifiable religious content to Woody's early years. As Mary Jo also recalls (and as was cited earlier): "We were ruled by Jesus and said the Lord's Prayer regularly. These rules set forth by our father, Charley, were embedded in us forever." (3)

Beyond being "ruled by Jesus" at home, and having such rule "embedded" in him, Woody could not help but be taken by the predominance of the figure of Jesus in the early 20th century rural Oklahoma culture into which he was born and raised. In that setting the presence of Jesus permeated the cultural atmosphere. Indeed, in the strong evangelical Protestant aura of that time and place, Jesus was pretty hard to miss whether or not one got up on a Sunday morning and got dressed for church. As Guthrie scholar Guy Logsdon observes, "He (Guthrie) could not divorce himself from his Oklahoma/Texas background in the Baptist and Church of Christ churches. Woody was a religious man, but not in the conventional sense." (4)

The Jesus figure, then, whom Woody had internalized at an early age remained with him throughout his life. New York City in 1940 was a long way from Okemah and Pampa in many more ways than one, but the Jesus whom Woody first encountered in those two small towns must have been much on his mind when he wrote *Jesus Christ*. As Woody himself tells it: "I wrote this song looking out of a rooming house window in New York City in the winter of 1940. I saw how the poor folks lived, and then I saw how the rich folks lived, and the poor folks down and out and cold and hungry, and the rich ones out drinking good whiskey and celebrating and wasting handfuls of money on gambling and women, and I got to thinking about what Jesus said, and what if He was to walk into New York City and preach like he used to. They'd lock him back in jail as sure as you're reading this. "Even as you've done it unto the least of these little ones, you have done it unto me." (5)

The passage Woody quotes is from the Gospel of Matthew, Chapter 25, Verse 40, where Jesus gives an account of how the Final Judgment will take place. However literally, or not, Woody took that story, he took the tune to *The Ballad of Jesse James* and wrote the following song:

> *Jesus Christ was a man who traveled through the land;*
> *a hard working man and brave.*
> *He said to the rich, "Give your money to the poor," But*
> *they laid Jesus Christ in his grave.*
> *Jesus was a man, a carpenter by hand. His followers*
> *were true and brave.*
> *One dirty little coward named Judas Iscariot laid Jesus*
> *Christ in his grave.*
> *He went to the preacher, he went to the sheriff. He told*
> *them all the same:*
> *"Sell all of your jewelry and give it to the poor," And*
> *they laid Jesus Christ in his grave.*
> *When Jesus came to town all the working folks around*
> *believed what he did say.*
> *But the bankers and the preachers, they nailed him on*
> *the cross, and they laid Jesus Christ in his grave.*
> *And the people held their breath when they heard about*
> *his death, everybody wondered why.*
> *It was the big landlord and the soldiers that they hired*
> *to nail Jesus Christ in the sky.*
> *This song was written in New York City, of rich man,*
> *preacher and slave.*
> *If Jesus was to preach like he preached in Galilee*
> *They would lay poor Jesus in his grave.*

Woody is largely drawing here on the Gospel story of the rich young man (a first century Palestine yuppie?) who asks Jesus what he must do to find fulfillment in this life. Jesus tells the young man to divest himself of his wealth and come follow him (Luke 18: 18-23). As is the case with many of the stories and parables in the Jesus Narrative, this one is open to a range of interpretation. Did Jesus really mean that the guy was to completely get rid of his entire earthly fortune and take up the vagabond life that Jesus and his disciples were living? Or was Jesus trying to make the larger point that the pursuit of earthy wealth will only get you so far when it comes to finding some deeper meaning to your life? The story, as told in the Gospel of Luke, is cryptic enough that either conclusion, along with various others, are possible.

Whatever Woody himself may have taken the story's meaning to be, he used it as one of the many ways in which he highlighted the plight of the poor in the midst of a land of plenty. His references to the "preachers" the "sheriff" and the "bankers"—the Biblical priests, Pharisees, and money-changers—point to what he (Guthrie) saw as the prevailing power structure's stacked deck against the underclass of both first century Palestine as well as mid-twentieth century America. And anyone who seriously challenges this power structure does so at the risk of his or her life, be it in America or in Galilee: "If Jesus was to preach like he preached in Galilee, they would lay poor Jesus in his grave." Whether or not one completely accepts Woody's take on the matter here, it is quite clear from this song, and others like it, that Woody Guthrie's social consciousness was shaped in good measure by his understanding of, and identification with, the life and times of Jesus of Nazareth.

This points to one of the many ironies, or paradoxes, in Woody's life: His attraction to the life and teachings of Jesus and his attraction, for a time, to the Communist Party came from the same piece of cloth. Whether it was Christianity or Communism, Woody had little use for ideology or doctrine in either realm. He first "met Jesus," so to speak, in the years leading up to the struggles of the Dust Bowl, followed by the Depression, in rural Oklahoma and Texas. His first encounters with the Communist Party were in the greater Los Angeles area—also in the Depression Era—when his saw his fellow Oklahomans and Texans, among others, desperately trying to eke out an existence in the agricultural fields of southern California. This was when and where he first met Will Geer, and largely through Geer's arrangements began singing at Party rallies. While the official Marxist party line may have held that religion is the "opiate of the people," Woody never felt he had to give up Jesus for the sake of following the party line. He saw the same ultimate goals being present in both the Jesus Narrative and in the dictates of socialism/ communism. However naïve, or not, he may have been on this score, the point is that when it came to Guthrie's religious consciousness and his political awareness, each one fed on the other. In expressing his admiration, for example, for Eugene Debs, the Socialist Party's five time Presidential candidate, Woody said of Debs that, he was a "pure mixture of Abraham Lincoln and Jesus."(6) Woody was only eight years old when Debs made his last run for President in 1920—from a jail cell, no less— but what he knew of Mr. Debs caused Woody to place him in his personal pantheon with Jesus and Abraham Lincoln. In writing his song *Christ for President*, Woody's mind may have been going back and forth between Eugene Debs and the Man from Galilee:

> *Let's have Christ for President. Let's have Him for our king.*
> *Cast your vote for the Carpenter that you call the Nazarene*
> *The only way you can ever beat these crooked political men*
> *Is to run the money-changers out of the temple*
> *And put the Carpenter in.*
> *O it's Jesus Christ our President; God above our King—*
> *With a job and a pension for the young and old, we will make hallelujah ring!*
> *Every year we waste enough to feed the ones who starve;*
> *We build our civilization up, and we shoot it down with wars.*
> *But with the Carpenter on the seat, away up in the capital town*
> *The USA will be on the way—prosperity bound!*

These are hardly the kind of words that a doctrinaire Communist would write and sing. They reflect more of a blend of religious sentiments and socialist utopianism: "A job and a pension for the young and old, we will make hallelujah ring!" The man who introduced Woody to the Communist Party, the aforementioned actor Will Geer, acknowledged as much: "He (Guthrie) was just a socialist instead of being an extreme Marxist. He was more of a Eugene Debs type. He certainly wasn't a Stalinist."(7)

Woody, by most accounts, did not combine his identification with the person of Jesus and his attraction to Debs' brand of socialism until he was well beyond Okemah and Pampa; but that blend was also in the cultural atmosphere of Guthrie's early years. In his definitive biography of Woody Guthrie, *Ramblin' Man,* Ed Cray describes this blend of socialism and frontier Christianity:

"Protestantism ran deep on the Western frontier, 'an enveloping ideology that gave meaning to the world of the country folk,' wrote historian Garin Burbank. It succored the poor in their misery and celebrated the rich in their success, explained good and evil as God's mysterious ways and comforted both the rich and the poor in dark times.

"Many prairie socialists found it hard to entirely throw over the old faith for the atheistic new. Instead they melded the two, arguing that socialist reform would lead to the Kingdom of Christ . . . .

"Socialism in Oklahoma became 'the primitive gospel of applied Christianity.' Onetime Presbyterian elder O.E. Enfield, a recent convert to socialism, assured readers of the *Ellis County Socialist* that he wanted to be called 'comrade.' 'There is [he said] only one title at the sound of which my heart throbs with greater joy, and that is the word 'Christian.'"(8)

Dr. Cray does not specifically say whether or not Woody had any direct encounters with this kind of Christian Socialism during his Okemah/Pampa years, but as just noted, it was one component of the religious and cultural atmosphere of those days. It is not known if Woody Guthrie ever came across a copy of the *Ellis County Socialist,* or ever heard of Presbyterian Elder Enfield, but the characterization of socialism in Oklahoma, circa the early 20th century, as "the primitive gospel of applied Christianity" is an apt description of Guthrie's dual attraction to the life and teachings of Jesus, and the goals—as he perceived them—of the Communist Party. That "primitive gospel of applied Christianity" is what clearly comes through in Woody's *Christ for President*.

A great irony in all of this is that one of the most vehement and outspoken opponents of Christian Socialism—or any form of socialism for that matter—was Woody's father, Charley Guthrie. As an active player, and occasional minor office holder, in the Democratic Party of his day, Charley appears to have taken it upon himself to be on a mission from God to see that the party was free from any kind of socialist infestation. After the Socialist Party had demonstrated some strength in Okemah's Okfuskee County, Charley Guthrie published a series of letters in the *Okemah Ledger*, beginning in the fall of 1911, to warn the populace. One such letter was titled, "Socialism—The Enemy of the Christian Religion." (9)

In March of 1912, three months prior to Woody's birth, Charley gathered up his Letters to the Editor and self-published them in a booklet he titled "Kumrids." Using some Biblical imagery he introduces his book in this manner: "The purpose of this little book is to give the reader an idea of the dangerous and poisonous fangs of the tempting serpent which is lurking behind the advancing claims of socialism." (10)

At a later point in this Introduction Charley says, "In discussing the Christian-Socialist question I will undertake to show that the name 'Christian' cannot well be placed as a prefix to 'socialism.'" (11)

What especially ignited Charley's ire was a visit to Okemah in that same year of 1912 by a Rev. Thurman (first name and religious affiliation are not available) who spoke on behalf of the Socialist Party in that election year. Thurman was advocating for the compatibility of socialism and the teachings in the Christian Gospels. In response to Rev. Thurman's speech in Okemah, Charley ran an article in the local newspaper titled: "Evasive, Shifting and Inconsistent: A Careful Diagnosis of the Socialist and Anti-Christian Speech Made in this City on Christmas Day by Agitator Thurman." (12)

An in-depth analysis of Charley Guthrie's strong anti-socialism is beyond the scope of this work. But a curious factor here is that the elder Guthrie lived until 1956, which means he lived to witness his son's adult life and career, along with the measure of fame that did come to Woody. By 1956 Woody had already been diagnosed with Huntington's chorea, and had been hospitalized, off and on, with the disease for four years. Charley must have been acquainted with his son's views, which combined his admiration for the life and teachings of Jesus with his socialistic leanings, and his Communist Party involvements. Yet there is no record that this writer can detect of any kind of conversation or interaction or exchange of opinions that Woody and Charley Guthrie might have had about their highly conflicting views on any kind of relationship between the teachings of Jesus and the tenets of socialism.

Charley and Woody may have found common ground, however, in their favorable views of the labor movement. In the same piece in which he attacked Rev. Thurman, Charley also pointed out that the Socialist Party had not provided the working man with as many benefits as the two million member American Federation of Labor—casting the AFL in a very favorable light.(13) Charley Guthrie did have a feel for the plight and the rights of working class men and women. But he did not extend those feelings to an embrace of socialism, much less see a connection between the teachings of Jesus and the tenets of socialism in the way that his son did.

A good case can be made, then, that Woody Guthrie's veneration of Jesus of Nazareth was one of the factors that held him back from an unqualified embrace of Communist Party dogma—along with his general aversion to dogmas of all kind. Woody very likely felt a mystical kind of identity with that "hard working man and brave" who traveled about the land of his day, attempting to bring an empowering message of hope and courage to the societal outcasts he deliberately chose to cast his lot with.

The men and women whom Woody considered to be "his people," basically occupied the same social and economic strata in the America of the 1920s, 30s, and 40s as did those of whom

Jesus in his day said, "Blessed are the poor for they shall inherit the Kingdom of God." Woody's vision was that of a more earth bound "Kingdom" for the dispossessed of his day, and he strongly believed that their rightful inheritance was a fair share of a land that was made for you and me.

In this sense Woody resonated well with the proponents of the Social Gospel of the early 20th century, who took seriously the line from the Lord's Prayer that says, "Thy Kingdom come, thy will be done, *on earth* (emphasis added) as it is in Heaven." That was part of Woody Guthrie's vision and calling—to bring to earth the "Kingdom" that Jesus said rightly belonged to the poor. He may not have regarded himself as "Mister Jesus," but Woody did see himself as one who was attempting to bring the same message—in its early twentieth century American version—that Jesus had brought to those whom he called "the least of these, my brethren."

CHAPTER FIVE

Woody the Theologian

The story of the life of Woody Guthrie is a study in paradoxes. One such paradox is that of a very intelligent, quick-witted, and well read individual (even without his having a high school diploma) who, at those times when it suited his purposes, liked to present himself as an aw-shucks country bumpkin. Journalism Professor Matthew Blake points up this paradox with respect to Woody's dealings with the Communist Party in the 1930s. (*Woody Guthrie: A Dust Bowl Representative in the Communist Party Press.* Journalism History. Winter, 2010). Blake points to Woody's deliberate phonetic misspellings in his *People's World* entries, i.e. "Woody Sez," with this observation: "With his phonetic spelling and composition, he implicitly portrayed himself as not formally educated, a depiction not entirely accurate . . . In his 1939 newspaper writings he also explicitly celebrated his purported ignorance and lack of education when addressing figures in business and journalism." Blake later adds, "While framing himself as uneducated, Guthrie's personal anecdotes and community folklore provided his audience with an informal dust bowl narrative." (1)

Woody, that is to say, was not one for turning out turgid tomes of Marxist theory which would mostly be read and discussed by other socialist intellectuals. He simply told his stories and sang his songs with a deliberate—but still authentic—kind of folksiness, and left it to his hearers and readers to draw out whatever kind of political theory might have been embedded in them. It was in good measure his unwillingness or inability to firmly attach himself to, or become a spokesperson for, any kind of doctrinaire political theory that prevented him from ever becoming a Communist Party apparatchik. With Woody Guthrie it was people first, and how the severe economic conditions of their time and place were affecting their lives. He was focused on singing his songs and telling his stories, and left the theoretical machinations to others.

There is a similar process at work when it comes to Woody the Theologian. It's an open question as to whether or not Woody Guthrie would have even embraced the designation of "theologian," as he was no more an academic theologian than he was an academic Marxist. He did, however, refer to himself as a "Soul Doctor." And in his letter to Effie Holladay following the death of his daughter Cathy he wrote, as we've seen, "I am a student of all faiths and creeds . . ." But, as was the case when it came to political theory, Woody Guthrie never set forth an explicit and systematic kind of theology. Here, too, he simply wrote what he had to say, and sang his songs, and let whatever theological content they may have contained emerge on its own and speak for itself.

Theology: The term literally means "knowledge of God," or "words (logos) about God." The word "religion" also breaks out into two components with Latin roots: "Re" meaning again (as in re-peat); and "ligare" which means to bind together. It's the same Latin root as the word ligament. Taken together these components provide the root meaning of the word religion: To bind together again. Religion, therefore, is the search for some underlying, unifying, and binding principle in our lives. In a larger sense religion is the human quest to re-turn to our original one-ness with all of being, with the entire Universe.

Theology, to follow this thread, is the language we use, inadequate and short of the mark as it will always be, when we attempt to give voice to the religious quest. From this angle we are all theologians at one time or another; times, that is to say, when we look up from the day-to-day-ness of our day-to-day lives and wonder about what greater meaning or purpose there might be to our lives; and how we might speak of that Greater Purpose, however we may choose to name it.

Even if the term "God" is problematic for some, we all still engage in theology. As one of my colleagues in the Unitarian Universalist ministry, the late Reverend Dr. Forrest Church wisely observed: "God is not God's name; it is my name for that which is greater than all and present in all." Dr. Church's words echo those of one the 20th century's most prominent theologians, Dr. Paul Tillich, who referred to G-o-d as "That Which Is Greater Than You Know, and Whose Name You Cannot Know."

Scattered throughout the writings and songs of Woody Guthrie we can see his own religious and spiritual quest: His own search for that which is greater than all and present in all; his own search for that which ultimately bound his life together and gave it a Greater Purpose. Whether he ever heard of Paul Tillich or not, Woody also probably knew that God was not God's name. But "God" was a term he often invoked, nonetheless. Woody Guthrie clearly had his own knowledge of God, and he put forth many words about God as he attempted to give voice to that knowledge.

It's not always the same God he writes or sings about. At times Woody's God is a very personal one to whom he makes very personal entreaties. At other times his God is more of a force or power or presence that one senses, and internalizes, but not necessarily forms an actual personal relationship with. While one does not find a consistent theology (i.e. words about God) in Woody's songs and writings, the more important point is that the varying theologies that do emerge from his works all point to a series of markers in an ongoing spiritual journey, with its many twists and turns, that made up the larger narrative of the life of Woody Guthrie.

At some points on his journey he keeps it pretty simple and straightforward by equating God with Love, as in this passage from *Born to Win*:

"Love is the only God I'll ever believe in. The books of the Holy Bible never say but one time just exactly what God is, and in those three little words it pours out a hundred million college educations and says, God Is Love. And that is the only real definite answer to ten thousand wild questions and queries that I myownself tossed at my Bible. I mean to say, that is the only really sensible, easy, honest, warm, plain, quick, and clear answer I found—*when I was ready to throw so-called fearful cowardly thieving poisoning religion out my back door* (emphasis added) it was these three words that made not only religion, but also several other sorts of superstitious fears and hatreds in me meet one very quick death. God Is Love. God is really Love."(2)

As we see here Woody had something of a love/hate relationship with religion itself. He quite rightly sees how religion can be—and, often, tragically is—"fearful, cowardly, thieving (and) poisoning." Some of his more caustic barbs are aimed at preachers, no less, like this comment: "Some of the preachers that promise you hamburgers in the hereafter get on my nerves; what I'd really like to do part of the time is to give 'em a hunk of black berry pie right in the face." (3) Woody wrote these words as a way of introducing a song he sang on occasion, and that was written by Joe Hill, titled *Pie in the Sky.* It is set to the tune of an old gospel number, *In the Sweet By and By,* and goes (in part):

> "Long-haired preachers come out every night;
> Try to tell you what's wrong and what's right.
> But when asked how 'bout something to eat, they will
>   answer in voices so sweet:
> 'You will eat, by and by, in that glorious land in the sky
> Work and pray, live on hay,
> You'll get pie in the sky when you die . . .
> If you fight hard for children and wife,
> Try to get something good in this life,
> You're a sinner and bad man they tell,
> When you die you will sure go to hell.'" (4)

As was often the case, Woody—with a little help from Joe Hill in this song—is using some down-home folksiness to work in a little political theory. The Marxist critique of religion was that it's an "opiate" used by the ruling class to keep the underclass in check by seducing them into believing that if they will only submit and persevere in this earthly life they will be rewarded in some Great Beyond.

Woody Guthrie did not dispute this critique; and he, no doubt, took a certain delight in using Joe Hill's words. But neither did he regard the Marxist critique as being the last word on religion. Woody did see a positive side to the religious quest. He did see a redeeming and saving feature in the religious search when it brings one to the revelation, as it was brought to him, that God Is Love.

The "God is Love" lines, as cited above, are found in the early pages of a chapter in *Born to Win* titled "My Secret." The chapter itself constitutes what can best be described as a Love Sermon. There are, however, no more references to God after these early paragraphs. But there are a great number of sentences, running over the course of several pages that begin with the word "Love," and in which the terms "Love" and "God" could be used interchangeably given the way Woody has set things up. These are only a few examples:

"Loves casts out hate.

Love gets rid of all fears.

Love washes all clean.

Love forgives all debts.

Love heals all.

Love is universal.

Love moves and balances every other planet star you see that are above you by the uncounted blue jillions.

And love causes peace and harmony to whirl a whole new universe on the inside of every atom."(5)

The lines in this chapter, as they go on from page to page, read like the cadences of a tent revival preacher who is on a roll; a style of preaching Woody was no doubt quite familiar with. Indeed, in some of the commentary he writes in *Hard Hitting Songs for*

Hard Hit People, Woody refers to "the hundreds and hundreds of testimonial services I've went to in Gospel Missions and the little Tent Churches all over the country."(6) He even works his way around to his own "come to Jesus" appeal as he winds his sermon down:

"And you of the deathly dope drug, you of the crazy needle, the reefer fag, the hot spoon, the opee (opium) pipe, the dead mattress, the gone spirit, the gone life . . . the spitty lips, the loud yells of choking sickness . . . your own fears and hates can be cured and healed up by one kind of love tonic; and one kind alone. Love will take your hand and lead you back . . ."(7) This is nothing less than a "Come to Love" altar call!

Woody may have meant it at the moment when he wrote that "Love is the only God I'll ever believe in," but in other places he goes well beyond his "God is Love" formula. His theology actually moves in a variety of directions, and sets down in variety of locations. While he probably never encountered the term "panentheism," there are certain of Woody's songs that reflect this type of theology. Panentheism posits God as a Sacred or Divine or Holy Presence that both engulfs, and is contained within, the natural world and universe. It is distinguished from pantheism, which equates all of existence with God, by holding that there is a sacred and holy dimension, or quality, to be found within existence. While pantheism makes God synonymous with the world and universe, panentheism holds out the promise and possibility that evidence of the sacredness of all life is contained within the world and universe; and that this sacredness is revealed to us on occasion.

In a well known passage from his book *Out of My Life and Thought* Albert Schweitzer recounts being on a barge on an African river in the summer of 1915, and being lost in thought as he pondered some overarching affirmation of life that would tie it all together for him: "At sunset (as) we were making our way through a herd of hippopotamuses there flashed upon my mind, unforeseen and unsought, the phrase "Reverence for Life." While, like Woody Guthrie, Schweitzer did not use the term, he is describing a "panentheistic moment" here: A moment, that is to say, when an awareness of the sacredness of life, and an awareness of its reverential nature, breaks through and into our human consciousness—often "unforeseen and unsought."

Two (out of several that could be cited) of Woody Guthrie's songs reflect his own panentheistic moments. These lyrics are from *Holy Ground*, which draw upon the legend of Moses and the burning bush as told in Hebrew scripture They were set to music by Frank London of the Klezmatics:

Take off take off your shoes
This place you're standing is holy ground . . .
These words I heard in my burning bush
This place you're standing, it's holy ground
This place you tread is holy ground.
God made this place this holy ground.
I heard my fiery voice speak to me
This spot you're standing, it's holy ground.

Woody then universalizes the experience as he moves from "This place" to:

Every spot on earth I traipse around
Every spot I walk is holy ground.
Every spot it's holy ground
Every little inch it's holy ground
Every grain of dirt it's holy ground
Every spot I walk is holy ground.

Another Guthrie song with panentheistic overtones is *This Morning I am Born Again*. It was set to music by Slaid Cleaves:

*This morning I was born again and a light shines on
   my land*
I no longer look for heaven in your deathly distant land
*I do not want your pearly gates, don't want your streets
   of gold,*
*This morning I was born again and a light shines on
   my soul.*
*This morning I was born again, my past is dead and
   gone.*
This great eternal moment is my great eternal dawn.
Each drop of blood within me, each breath of life I breathe
*Is united with these mountains and these mountains
   with the sea.*
I feel the sun upon me, its rays crawl through my skin.
I breathe the life of Jesus and old John Henry in.
*I give myself, my heart, my soul to give some friend a
   hand*
*This morning I am born again; I am in the promised
   land.*

The promise of panentheism is that however fallen and broken and despoiled it may be, this world, this life, this here-and-now is also the "promised land" if we can see and sense it as such. If such an awareness could ever become widespread enough, if we as a human race could ever reach the point where we fully recognize that every drop of blood within us "is united with these mountains and the mountains with the sea" perhaps the human race, and the world it occupies would have a chance after all. Whether it's ever fully realized or not we can thank Woody Guthrie for holding up the promise.

However much certain of his songs may be reflective of certain schools of theology, Woody Guthrie—being Woody Guthrie—did not write any of his more religiously oriented works within the confines of any one belief system. In what we've seen to this point of Woody's God, It is more of a Power or Force or Presence than a willful or intentional Being. But there are other "God writings" of Guthrie's that go in a more personal direction and make more personal kinds of references and appeals to a Deity.

One of the more poignant songs of this genre is *God's Promise*. While the name of God is never invoked in the song itself the title assumes, or strongly suggests, that Woody is taking on the voice of God in *God's Promise*. It is set to music by Ellis Paul:

> I didn't promise you skies painted blue
> Not colored flowers all your days through.
> I didn't promise you sun with no rain;
> Joys without sorrows, peace without pain.
> All that I promise is strength for this day,
> Rest for my worker and light on your way.
> I give you truth when you need it, my help from above,
> Undying friendship, my unfailing love.
> I never did promise you crowns without tears
> Food with no hard sweat, your tears without smiles
> Hot sunny days without cold wintry snows
> No vict'ry without fightin', no laughs without woes
> I sure didn't say I'd give you heaven on earth,
> A life with no labor, no struggles, no deaths,
> No earthquakes no dryspells, no fire flames, no droughts,
> No slaving, no hungers, no blizzards, no blights.
> I promise you power, this minute this hour
> The power you need when you fall down to bleed.
> I give you my peace and my strength to pull home
> My love for all races, all creeds, and all kinds.

The God Woody is offering here is clearly not a pie-in-the-sky kind of Deity who can always promise to make everything all right. At the same time it is a God who is willfully engaged with human beings and who provides a source of strength in times of trial and trouble. There is more going on in this song than the Sacred Presence of panentheism, comforting as that can be. There is no negation of panentheism here, but there is a moving beyond it. It is a movement from a Presence to a Being who speaks directly to human beings in our brokenness and failings, and offers us the strength to pursue hope and wholeness.

This is not a God of any one faith or particular persuasion, as the closing lines indicate:

My flavors, my saviors, my creeds of all kinds,

My love for my saviors, all colors all kinds,

My love for my races, all creeders, all kinds,

But He, She, or It is a God who personally reaches out with a message of hope and promise to all persons of faith, whatever their faith may be. We'll pick up this thread in the chapter on "Woody the Universalist."

Be it the Power of Love, the Presence of the Sacred or Holy, or a more personal Deity who offers strength in times of need, Woody touched all of these bases as he attempted to offer his own words and wisdom—his own "logos," if you will—of God. He didn't have to be consistent in his theology; consistency of thought and theory wasn't one of his hallmarks anyway. What Woody the Theologian does offer are various ways of being a believer; not a believer in a particular creed or doctrine of God but a believer in the hope and possibilities of Life. He had a gifted way of using God language, language very familiar to many of the listeners he was trying to reach, in a way that could lift them up and set their sights somewhere beyond the often dreary nature of their daily lives, and allow them to see that they were indeed a part of Something Greater than themselves.

It was this reaching for a Greater Connection that also provided the underpinnings for the kinds of union organizing and activity that Woody and his comrades also strove to promote. He was hardly shy about invoking his religion, his "knowledge of God" (theology) when it came to his union activities. In a commentary on the song *One Big Union* Guthrie makes a direct appeal to religion in stating his case for unionism: "One Big Union has got to come. You believe it. I know you do. You believe it because the bible says You'll all be one with the Father. That is as High as Religion goes. Then over there somewhere it says God is Love. So you see that the reason you got Religion is so's everybody can All be One in Love . . . I studied religion 6 years, and prayed some days for hours, and talked to lots of folks every day about living and loving and giving. That's religion. That's Real Religion: Living, Loving, and Giving."(8)

It was in his later, and very tragic years, that Woody's attraction to religion and his understandings of God took their most personal turn. This will be dealt with more fully in a later chapter, but bears touching upon here. From the time of his initial hospitalizations for Huntington's Disease in 1952 Woody wrote voluminously for as long as his physical abilities allowed him to do so. As the effects of Huntington's became increasingly acute he eventually got to the point were he could no longer hold a pen or pencil. But before he reached that point he produced some of his most poignant writing as he struggled to come to terms with his life, and with the disease that was slowing taking his life from him.

As the year 1954 came to a close, with Woody in Brooklyn State Hospital, he turned out a twenty three page, hand written document which he titled "My Bible." Even at this time, nearly twelve years before his death, his handwriting was already becoming difficult to read. But here's one small portion of what Woody wrote (and the punctuation and spelling is as he wrote it): "I just stand here and I say that if there's not any godly father above me then my humanly life . . . just isn't worth living. My mother father God's words and all of his Godly goodly promise to me are all that makes me keep on walking."(9)

We cannot know whether or not Woody Guthrie was recalling the song he'd written years earlier—*God's Promise*—when he says that "God's goodly promise to me are all that makes me keep on walking," but the song certainly speaks to the struggles of Woody's final years:

"I didn't promise you skies painted blue; Not colored flowers all your days through.

I didn't promise you sun with no rain; Joys without sorrows, peace without pain.

All that I promise is strength for this day; Rest for my worker and light on your way."

For all of the words about God that Woody Guthrie wrote over the course of his life, this is what it finally came down to: A reaching out for a promise and source of strength before this indefatigable worker for peace and justice found his final rest. And he left a lot of light in his way.

CHAPTER SIX

Woody the Universalist

"So much is going on in the world. Everything and everybody is a potential story or a song. Life, the universe is a great symphony and the stars, planets, the earth and us people are just one great dance. These are the things that are on my mind."(1) These are a few lines from an amazing, and amazingly long, letter Woody Guthrie wrote to Marjorie Greenblatt Mazia, dated June 11, 1944. By now Woody and Marjorie had already seen the birth of their daughter Cathy, but they would not be married until the fall of the following year, in November of 1945.

The letter was written while Woody was on ship in the United States Merchant Marine as he served in that capacity during World War II. (Whether he was aware of it or not, his letter was written during the week following D-Day.) Taken as a ratio of casualties to the number of enlistees, the Merchant Marine actually had the highest death rate of all the Service branches in the Second World War. Those serving on the ships may have been "non-combatants," but their lives were at great risk from torpedo attacks. So it was at a time when his life was the most vulnerable, and the most expendable, that Woody poured out his thoughts to Marjorie about what he repeatedly refers to as the "One Union" or "One Big Union."

There is very little in this letter that Woody had not expressed in other places and in other ways when it comes to his views on religion, and their links to his union activities. When it comes to this one letter, however, what is both remarkable, and extremely helpful when it comes to an exploration of Guthrie's spirituality, is that it captures much of Woody's wide ranging thought in a single document. For all of his on-board ship duties, and for all of his interactions with his shipmates, Woody also had a lot of time on his hands for thinking and writing. So there's a lot he pulls together here in what could be called his "Oneness Letter" or his "One Big Union" letter to Marjorie.

Woody, no doubt, took the phrase "One Big Union" from his years of involvement in the labor struggles of the 1930s and early 40s. It was a concept and slogan that emerged in the late 19th and early 20th centuries in various sectors of the trade union movement, principally with the International Workers of the World, also known as "The Wobblies." In 1911, one year before Woody's birth, the IWW put out a widely circulated pamphlet and booklet using the title "One Big Union." What Woody does in this letter to Marjorie is to take a well known and much used rallying cry from the labor movement and give it a decidedly spiritual and universalistic dimension: "The universe is a great symphony (a great union?), and the stars, planets, the earth, and us people are just one great dance."(2)

The letter itself, with its 21 handwritten pages, moves back and forth between specific reportage type descriptions of what's happening around him on the ship, to Woody's religious, philosophical, and spiritual meanderings and explorations on the theme of "One Union" or "Oneness" as he also calls it. What apparently triggered his thoughts was a sermon by the ship's Chaplain as described on the third page:

"Yesterday the chaplain preached us a sermon about Moses. About a very great man." Moving from Moses, Woody offers his take on the Psalms: "Now these Psalms are very great and beautiful

flights of the human mind recorded in the forms of writing."(3)
Taking off on that thought, Woody shifts into his own flight of the
human mind with his own form of writing:

"As a general rule any activity of the mind which tends to show
us the real 'Oneness' of all things is great. The more a song shows
us this Oneness the greater is that song. This is the highest activity
of your mind and heart, this Oneness. To see and to feel and to
know of this Oneness, this Union, is to see the relation and the
connection between all objects, forces, peoples, and creatures."(4)

At another place in the letter he combines theology, trade
unionism, and a bit of American history all in one mix:

"I was talking (earlier) of Moses and Abraham and the thought
of monotheism versus polytheism. Polytheism means the worship
of many gods. Monotheism (is) the belief in only one god. Now I
see all of this very plain but I simply try to put these same thoughts
or concepts into the history of the trade unions. Some people
believe in many things and many unions separate and distinct
from one another. I simply believe in mono-unionism, in One Big
Union which includes all people and all things. This is the state of
the Union for which Tom Paine fought and for which Abraham
Lincoln lived and died . . . . This Union is not only possible but is an
actual fact. It is alive and living in the people all around you."(5) He
picks up this thread a few pages later with this observation: "This
is why all great religions preach the central idea of Oneness."(6)

There are two modes of universalism that come through in the
writings and songs of Woody Guthrie. They each find expression
in this letter. While the two modes have their overlapping features
they are also quite distinct. There is "cosmic universalism" that
affirms the relatedness of all things in the universe, the relatedness
of all of Being. It was this cosmic universalism that provided the
spiritual underpinning for Woody's indefatigable efforts on behalf
of union organizing. But his union advocacy was, in the end,
spiritual work and a spiritual quest that went well beyond any
political theory or strategy.

Then there was a more specific kind of religious universalism
in which Woody sought out the truths that are common to the

various religious traditions of the world, leading him to say, as just shown above, "all great religions preach the central idea of Oneness." While his primary focus and identity remained with Christianity, or more specifically on his veneration of the person of Jesus, Woody came to appreciate the particularities of other religious faiths and discovered an underlying unity in them.

Taking his cosmic universalist mode first, in something of a mystical kind of way Woody could go from seeing a particular entity or object or activity and placing it in a Very Big Picture. Just prior to his Merchant Marine experience Woody did some random jottings from a home he had on Charles Street in New York City, giving them the title of *People are Words*. In part he writes: "This is why I say union. I would be a killer if I didn't talk union and walk union. I saw that the cells out here in my backyard bush could not be no bush if they'd not joined the other cells in union."(7)

What Woody is striving to articulate in these kinds of writings of his is a very simple and profound—all at the same time—concept. He's really writing about the interdependence of all existence or the interdependent web of all life; and about how each "piece" of existence is a reflection of what he calls "One Big Thing." While various theologians have written of this concept in largely academic language, Woody takes a more poetic approach, and these passages indicate:

"To see all of this (Oneness) in nature and in people, this was what caused the Hebrews to write psalms. It caused the Negroes to sing their work songs. It causes all of us to love and to sing praises in one way or another about our past in this endless infinite eternal march of human labors and historic events. It can be seen in a rock or in a bird on a limb or a lonesome sunset . . . This is a very big and vast thing. It is a thing so great that when it does come to you it fills you with such a power and energy that all things feel possible in your hands . . . all life is one to you. It all flows, rises, moves, vibrates as one to you." It is this Oneness that also, as Woody tells it, makes a common bond of humanity itself: "The sweat of the brow in Coney Island is the same sweat in South Africa, and the labor of a German farmer is connected with the Russian School Teacher."(8)

Woody is describing to Marjorie an experience, or series of experiences, that are common to most prophets, visionaries, and seers; that is to say, certain transformational moments that give them a glimpse of a Transcendent Reality; a Reality that is named by a wide variety of terms. Jesus' time in the wilderness prior to his earthly ministry and the Buddha meditating under the Bo Tree before embarking upon his earthly mission are two of the better known examples of this phenomenon. It then becomes the life mission or calling of those who catch such a universalistic vision to try to convey something of its message and meaning to their fellow human beings. As seen in an earlier chapter, sometimes the possession of a vision of a transcendent reality can actually blind one to certain other on-the-ground realities that most mortals find themselves having to deal with. I refer to this as the "Holy Paradox."

The role of such a prophet then, who has had his or her vision of cosmic universalism, is to try to interpret and place that universalism in whatever social and historical context he/she happens to be, and hopefully in a way that it can be at least be partially grasped by his/her hearers. This is why Jesus largely taught in parables, drawing on images and activities that were well known to the people of his time and place in order to convey a greater message about a God of universal love and justice.

Woody took much the same approach with his concept or vision of Oneness. He translated it into plainly sung and easily understood songs and sayings that were ultimately rooted in his idea of One Big Union. He alludes to this approach in this same letter to Marjorie:

"One more thing in regard to this idea of One Big Union. You of course don't have to have the idea shoved into your mouth. Most folks accept the broad general theory of One Big Something or Other; one Great Force; one First Principle; one Big Something. Not all of them know exactly what this One Big Thing is. They see their own little part or corner plain enough, know that their labors go on out toward winning a war or putting the nation on rubber tires or paint on houses."(9)

But then Woody goes on to maintain that having a piece of the picture doesn't always lead to grasping the whole picture: "Many people have never been taught nor have ever given much time to any sort of this type of thinking and naturally their life is based on some sort of greed. These are our gamblers and gangsters and robbers of all sorts. (But) many harmless, innocent, educated people become too wrapped up in their own little selves and so they do not learn about this greater union of us."(10) Woody then extends this critique even to some of those involved in the trade union movement itself:

"I have met so called brilliant thinkers who are blinded in one way or more and who will deny all of this as foolish, mystic superstitions speculation. Many people who are actually engaged in organizing trade unions do not see this whole concept."(11) Very interesting. Woody even takes to task here some of his apparent comrades-in-arms in the labor organizing movement for still having a less than holistic vision of what the calls "this whole concept." There is a strong suggestion in just these two sentences as to why Woody Guthrie was not quite able, in the end, to fully embrace the doctrines or dogma of the Communist Party, even though he shared many of its goals; and worked, wrote, and sang on the Party's behalf for a good part of his life. A similar point along this line was made in the "Woody and Jesus" chapter. Woody does not identify the "brilliant thinkers," and he does not single out those in the trade union movement as those who "do not see this whole concept." One can only speculate as to who he had in mind in this part of his letter. My guess is that he was referring to those who were equating the attainment of One Big Union with the full and final implementation of a socio-economic-political theory. Were his "brilliant thinkers" doctrinaire, academic Marxists who believed that if their theory could only be fully actualized then utopia would be attained? Again, one can only speculate.

In Woody's case he was embracing the largely secular idea of One Big Union, a la the trade unions, while also seeking to move beyond it to a more spiritual realm. He knew his political theory, but above and beyond political theory Woody Guthrie was also hearing a voice that was chanting that this land, this world, this universe was made for you and me. For all of our worldly divisions we are a part of a mystical body of union. Woody knew this. Indeed, as he notes, there were those—some of them, no doubt, his comrades in the trade unions—who "will deny all this as foolish, mystic superstitious speculation." But he is really attempting to give voice to that which ultimately lies at the base of all of the world's religions—past, present, and future—which is the sense that we human beings are a part of something greater than ourselves that we cannot finally or adequately name, or finally and fully identify, but we know it's there. Perhaps Woody's labeling his concept of cosmic universalism as "The One Big Something or Other" is as good a term as any.

The second mode of Woody Guthrie's universalism, as previously noted, had to do with his finding truth and value in a variety of the world's religious traditions, i.e. his religious universalism. Recall once again his words to Jim Longhi while on the same Merchant Marine run as when he wrote his Oneness Letter: "Hell yes I'm a religious man. I kinda like them all."(12) And, again as well, in his letter to Effie Holladay after the death of his daughter Cathy: "I myself am a master and a student of all faiths and all creeds seeing the same general spiritual feelings and ideas present in them all."(13) Or these lyrics from his song *God's Promise:* "My flavors, my saviors, my creeds of all kinds; My love for my saviors, all colors all kinds; My love for my races, all creeders all kinds . . ."

Similar allusions to Woody's religious universalism are found scattered throughout the Oneness Letter. For example: "This whole sum and total has been called by a thousand names. The Chinese call it Yogism (sic) or 'Union' the Indians call it Prana or 'Energy,' the Mohammedans call it Allah, the Christians call it 'God' or 'good' or 'love.'"(14) Woody may not have gotten all the terminology completely correct here, but he's got the concept down well as he reiterates his earlier contention that "all great religions preach the central idea of Oneness."(14)

One of the great and horrible tragedies of human history, however, is that Woody was, at best, only half right when it comes to what all religions preach. When one considers all the wars that have been fought, all the human beings who have been tortured and/ or executed, all the lives that have been demeaned or destroyed— with so much of it all done in the name of religion—then one can only wonder just how true the assertion is that all religions preach "Oneness." The maddening irony here is that so often practitioners of one faith will claim that their idea of Oneness is superior to all others—sometimes to the point that "all others" must be, in one way or another, eliminated.

But, as just stated, the good news is that Woody may have been at least half right. Perhaps there is some hope in even that. Consider that the great divide in this present day, when it comes to the religions of the world, is not *between* the various faith traditions but *within* them. This divide within some of the world's faiths, particularly the monotheistic ones, is between the exclusivists and the universalists. The words are largely self-explanatory. The exclusivists hold that their faith is the one true one and those outside of it are infidels. The universalists see their faith as a piece of a larger whole, of a larger truth, that will probably never be fully known or realized, but can still be aspired towards. They see their particular faith as providing them a glimpse of a Larger Whole. These religious universalists do not deny that there are marked differences among the various religious faiths; but they also seek to look beyond these differences for the common ground that points us human beings in the direction of a greater awareness of our common humanity. Yes, Woody was right to say that "all great religions preach the idea of Oneness," but he needed to qualify his statement to say that it's really certain segments within these great religions that preach the idea of Oneness.

Continuing with this issue, some of what Woody wrote to Marjorie in 1944 about religious universalism found expression in a column in *The Boston Globe* in the fall of 2011 that was written by James Carroll. Carroll is a former priest, an author, and a commentator/columnist on religion in modern public life.

His October, 2011 *Globe* column was titled "Monotheism Doesn't Mean 'We're Number One.'" After citing certain contemporary incidents of religious bigotry within three of the world's major faiths, Carroll goes on to decry "what happens when the embers of earthly conflict are fanned into flames by the heavenly justification of a twisted monotheism." He then goes on to ask, "What if monotheism isn't about being number one? . . . To say, as the Book of Genesis does, that God is the creator of all that exists—and not just of the tribe—means that all creatures are alike in participating in God's life."(15)

Carroll then wraps up his piece with words that actually sound like a slightly re-written version of Woody's letter: "This vision of oneness is what launched the religion known as Judaism, what motivated Jesus, and what gripped Mohammad. If Judaism has survived through the millennia, and if both Christianity and Islam have seized the imaginations of multitudes, the core reason is not a spirituality of combat, but a belief in the promises of peace." In these few lines we have a contemporary religious scholar, and an interpreter of religion in contemporary culture, giving the distinct impression of channeling Woody Guthrie!

As already seen, Woody's religious universalism had its origins back during his late teens as he was working his way through the books in the Pampa, Texas library—especially the ones dealing with Western religions, Eastern philosophy, and the, then, newly published parables and saying of the Lebanese-American poet and mystic, Kahlil Gibran. His interest in Eastern mysticism stayed with him for much of his life thereafter.

One of the tensions in Woody's first marriage to Mary Jennings Guthrie, in addition to his abrupt departures and his philandering, was over the religious education of their children. Mary wanted then raised Catholic, in accordance with her own faith. While Woody was willing to be married in a Catholic ceremony, which did carry with it the promise and obligation of the children of that marriage being raised in the Catholic faith, he resisted this move when the time came. He wanted his offspring to adopt his more free thinking ways rather than being indoctrinated in a particular religious faith.

Then, as Woody was radicalized in his early California days to the plight and exploitation of the farm workers he encountered, he re-appropriated the person of Jesus. With Woody Jesus became less and less of a personal Lord and Savior—as proclaimed in the evangelical Protestantism of rural Oklahoma and Texas—and more of a "savior" of the working class. Jesus became Woody's ultimate working class hero. His continuing attachment to Christianity was bound up in this image of Jesus as his song "Christ for President" demonstrates. In his later, and tragically declining years, as will be shown in forthcoming chapters, Woody moved more and more into a particular, and somewhat mystical, embrace of Christ as Huntington's Disease slowly eroded his life.

It was his marriage to Marjorie, however, that moved him to deepen and strengthen his knowledge and appreciation of Judaism. Marjorie's parents were Jewish émigrés. Her mother, Aliza Waitzman, was from a region of Eastern Europe known as Bessarabia; her father, Isidore, was from Romania. They met, married, and raised their family in Philadelphia. Marjorie was a member of the Martha Graham Dance Company in New York, and married to Joseph Maiza, when she met Woody in February of 1942. While the Greenblatt's, especially Isidore, were largely secularized Jews, their home life was reflective of Jewish culture and they observed the Jewish Holy Days.

There was some initial reluctance on the part of Marjorie's parents when it came to their acceptance of Woody, especially in view of the fact that their daughter was already married. In time, however, the acceptance did come, even with the often tumultuous marriage that ensued. One outcome of their marriage, in addition to the four children they had, was Woody's attraction to, and even—to a point—identification with, Judaism. In an entry in a date book of his, dated January 5—10, 1946 Woody appears to connect with the religious culture of his spouse as he describes the area of Coney Island where they were living at the time: "Coney Island, where the Yiddish speak on the streets in a mountain voice . . . I stand here for a minute . . . and use my trick key to see Coney Island in the land of pure rhythm. I feel an ancient and modern rhythm here along these Jewish streets of people wise and friendly."(16) The "Jewish streets" have become his streets, and their rhythm becomes one that Woody feels for himself.

The ancient and modern rhythm Woody felt on those "Jewish streets" came to find expression in a whole genre of songs he wrote, both about Hanukkah, and ones like *Holy Ground* which drew upon Jewish tradition and imagery. In 2006 the New York City based musical group The Klezmatics, which were first organized in 1986, released two CDs of nothing but Woody Guthrie's songs from this genre titled *Woody's Wheel* and *Woody Guthrie's Happy Joyous Hanukkah*. The titles of the Hanukkah songs include: "Hanukah Bell," "Hanuka Tree," "Hanuka's Flame," and "Honeyky Hanuka." [The spellings are Woody's]

Behind his writing of songs such as these is Woody's clearly intentional effort to gain a deeper understanding of their religious and historical context. Contained in the Guthrie Archives are a couple of documents that demonstrate this. They are a couple of Jewish publications that Woody thoroughly peruses. The documents themselves were probably common and familiar within the Jewish communities of that time and place. One is titled *How to Celebrate Hanukah at Home* and published by the United Synagogues of America; the other appears to be a newsletter put out by the Jewish Education Committee of New York and titled *Suggestions for Hanukkah Programs*. The texts of these two items are just what their titles indicate. What's intriguing is all the underlining and marginal notes that Woody Guthrie made as he studied them. It's clear that he's making a dedicated effort to educate himself about the story behind the Celebration of Hanukkah, as well as the reasons for, and meanings of, the various elements and components of the Celebration. Above the title of the *How to Celebrate . . . .* booklet he writes in large letters, "Part of my worldly goods, Woody Guthrie." What all this suggests to me is that Woody wanted to avoid a cavalier appropriation of a religious tradition for the sake of a few songs; and that he wanted instead anything he wrote based on that tradition to come from a knowledgeable and appreciative understanding of it.

Woody Guthrie, then, was both a cosmic universalist and a religious universalist. He carried within himself a vision of the ultimate unity of all being—the Oneness of All Things as he called it. He carried within himself as well an awareness of an essential commonality among the religious faiths of humankind—that for all their differences "all religions preach this Oneness."

"This is the highest activity of your mind and heart, this Oneness . . . To see all the relations between all objects, forces, peoples, and creatures . . . This Union is alive and living in the people all around you."(17) So wrote Woody Guthrie even as he was working on a ship that was a part of a war effort in the deadliest war ever waged to that point in human history. A paradox, perhaps; but it's still striking that in the midst of one of humanity's greatest imperfections, that is to say the waging of war, Woody Guthrie was able to see beyond that imperfection to a greater truth. In the midst of the brokenness of conflict he held up a vision of Oneness.

Without, I hope, being too grandiose about it, I would say that the future well being of the human race, if not our very planet, stands or falls upon how well this vision becomes realized.

CHAPTER SEVEN

Woody Guthrie and the Holy Paradox

My two American heroes are Woody Guthrie and Jack Kerouac. There are a number of parallels to be found in looking at each of their lives. Woody and Jack were each drawn to the social and cultural outcasts of their day. Each of them felt a mystical connection to the American landscape that provided the backdrop against which these marginalized folks struggled for some kind of a meaningful existence. For Woody Guthrie the landscape was the America of the 1920s, 30s, and early 40s. For Kerouac it was the post World War II American landscape from the late 1940s through the early 1960s. Compare, by way of example, these two odes to America from each of their best known works:

These are the concluding lines of Jack Kerouac's *On the Road*:

"So, in America when the sun goes down and I sit on the old broken down river pier under the long, long skies of New Jersey and think of all that raw land that rolls in one unbelievable huge bulge over to the West Coast and all the people dreaming in the immensity of it . . . the evening star must be drooping and shedding her sparkler dims on the prairie which is just before the coming of the complete night that blesses the earth, darkens all the rivers, cups the peaks, and folds the final shore in . . ."[1]

And from Woody Guthrie signature song:

> I roamed and rambled and followed my footsteps
> To the sparkling sands of her diamond deserts.
> And all around me a voice was sounding, 'This land was
>   made for you and me . . .'
> As the sun came shining and I was strolling
> With the wheat fields waving and the dust clouds blowing
> As the fog was lifting a voice was chanting
> This land was made for you and me.

The captivating and panoramic descriptions of their native land which Kerouac and Guthrie offer in these passages come from a deeply held spiritual bond each man felt with his country even as they, each in their own way, engaged in a lover's quarrel with it. As just noted, both Guthrie and Kerouac felt a mystical connection to the persons who were living on the margins of this bountiful land. One of the definitions Kerouac gave to the word "beat" was that of persons who had been beaten out to the edges, or beaten down to the bottom, of American society. While Woody did not have such an all encompassing term as did Jack, he too regarded as "his people" those who had every good reason to question if they were, in fact, living in a land that was made for them. When it came to both the physical and cultural landscape of America, and the people living in it who Jesus termed "the least of these," Woody Guthrie and Jack Kerouac felt a very real, and yet unsentimental, kind of love.

Each man was also, again in his own way, quite religious. Kerouac retained, throughout his life, his devotion to the French-Canadian style of Roman Catholicism in which he was raised; while also—for a time—expanding his religious and spiritual awareness to an embrace of Buddhism. Woody Guthrie, as we've already seen, was raised in, and strongly influenced by, the aura of early 20th century rural American Protestantism, while going on to become a universalistic scholar of world religions, and expressing, "I sorta like them all." His self-described title of "The Soul Doctor" was one that fit him well.

Along with such ennobling traits, however, the lives of Woody Guthrie and Jack Kerouac are also marked by some very similar kinds of personal failings; failings, that is to say, according to the conventional standards of their day, and of ours. Jack Kerouac had two failed marriages, one of which produced a daughter whose existence he barely, and then grudgingly, acknowledged. His third marriage was to a woman who became, essentially, his nursemaid as he continued his losing battle with alcoholism and drank himself to death at age 47. When it came to being a family man, Woody Guthrie does come off somewhat better than Kerouac; while still leaving much to be desired.

Both Jack and Woody lived out the paradox of being brilliant individuals, who could be kind, gentle, compassionate, and loving souls at times; while at other times both were just plain damned hard—if not impossible—to live with. They each, as well, had their battles with the bottle. Both men, that is to say, were living examples of The Holy Paradox.

Woody Guthrie had a certain kind of holiness about him, to the point, as we've seen, that he was regarded by some as "Mister Jesus." He was a visionary and an artist. Holiness, as the term is being used here, however, needs to be distinguished from piety. There was very little in Woody Guthrie's life in the way of piety, that is to say in living one's life in strict accordance with supposedly divinely decreed rules and practices.

Holiness is another matter. Holiness connotes the ability or the wherewithal to see both through and beyond one's immediate surroundings and doings, and visualize a sacred dimension to Life with a capital 'L' It is to feel a mystical bond or a sacred connection with the Life that enfolds us all. As Woody himself put it in his song *Holy Ground*: "Every spot on earth I traipse around; Every spot I walk it's holy ground." And from *This Morning I am Born Again*: "This morning I was born again, I was born again complete. I stood above my troubles and I stand on my two feet. My hand it feels unlimited, my body feels like the sky. I feel at home in the universe where yonder planets fly." It takes a certain kind of holy consciousness, as well as an artistic consciousness, to know and record the experiences Woody describes here. The writings of Jack Kerouac are full of similar sentiments.

But then there's The Holy Paradox. It's the paradox that the day to day behavior of many persons who possess this holy consciousness seems, at times, to belie their vision. Some persons who are blessed (or could it be cursed?) with visionary and artistic sensitivities can at times behave towards other human beings in downright insensitive ways. Perhaps it was Marjorie Guthrie who best expressed this holy paradox when she very succinctly said about her husband: "I don't think it's possible for a person to be a great artist and a great human being."[2]

Well now, and with all due respect for Marjorie (which is considerable), Woody Guthrie was a great human being. He just wasn't always a good human being. His long time compadre, Pete Seeger, captured the distinction well when he noted, "I can't stand him when he is around, but I miss him when he's gone."[3] Allowing for a bit of hyperbole on Mr. Seeger's part, he is really speaking of how it's possible to love someone who is not always easy to like. Such were the challenges, and at times the trials, for those who knew Woody Guthrie best, i.e. loving someone dearly who could also, again at times, be hard to like. There are a myriad of stories that point up this dichotomy in the life of Woody Guthrie. This is just one from Ed Cray's biography *Ramblin' Man*:

"Guthrie was 'a hellion, an outlaw getting even with the big guys,' (Studs Terkel observed) . . . His rage against the Interests could be petty, even 'unpardonably rude' as Alan Lomax's gently reared sister Bess puts it. Invited with (fellow Almanac Singer Millard) Lampell to the expansive home of a friend of Lampell's, Guthrie was uncomfortable and grew hostile. He brazenly tried to pocket a cigarette lighter, then silverware, and a cigarette box. Each time the hostess snatched them back. Guthrie finally went off with a wedge of cheese and a bottle of brandy stuffed in his pockets . . . (Later) at a picnic in Milwaukee for Allis-Chalmers workers, Guthrie got drunk on 'Old Overcoat' . . . Lampell wrote that he hustled Guthrie away, hit him in the jaw, and then threw him stunned into the back seat of a Buick to sleep it off."[4]

Then there was the womanizing. To pick up the Kerouac/ Guthrie thread again for a moment, Jack Kerouac kept a list, which is dutifully preserved in the Kerouac Archive in the New York Public Library, of every woman he ever had sex with, noting the date(s) and place(s). Jack's is a pretty impressive, if that's the word, roll call. Woody wasn't the compulsive list maker that Kerouac was, but had he (Woody) been keeping a similar record of sexual conquests, his list would have rivaled, if not surpassed, that of Jack's.

This gets us to the matter of Woody Guthrie's families, his wives and children. But before putting the focus on the families Woody Guthrie brought forth, consider first the "family values" of two other visionaries who have left their indelible marks on our world.

In 1907 Mahatma Gandhi received a letter from his older brother, Laxmidas, taking him to task for not paying sufficient attention to his immediate family's well being. The family Laxmidas was referring to was Gandhi's wife and four children. Gandhi's reply was as follows: "I fail to understand what you mean by the word 'family' . . . If I could say so without arrogance I would say that my family now comprises all living beings."[5] All living beings or not, four years later Gandhi's eldest son, Harilai, would renounce his familial ties to his acclaimed father. This move was but one indication of Gandhi's often tenuous, and rather mysterious at times, relationship with his immediate family even as he was gaining global recognition for his moral leadership in India.

Some nineteen hundred years earlier another great prophet and lover of humanity expressed similar sentiments. The 13th chapter of the Gospel of Matthew offers this account from the life of Jesus of Nazareth: "While he (Jesus) was speaking to the crowd his mother and brothers appeared outside, wishing to speak to him. Someone told him, 'your mother and brother are standing outside asking to speak with you.' But he said in reply to the one who told him, 'Who is my mother? Who are my brothers?' And stretching his hand towards his disciples he said, 'here are my mother and my brothers. For whoever does the will of my heavenly Father is my brother and sister and mother.'"

There's the paradox again; in this case of persons who feel a spiritual connection to the great swath of humankind while having difficulty living out that connection with those for whom they are supposedly the closest, and for whom they bear the greatest responsibility. Putting Woody Guthrie in the company of Gandhi and Jesus Christ might seem a bit of a stretch, but when applying the holy paradox to family matters the comparison holds.

In October of 1933 twenty-one year old Woody Guthrie married sixteen year old Mary Jennings in Pampa, Texas. He and Mary's brother, Matt, had become good friends and musical collaborators. Mary and Woody would have three children in the following six years. Theirs was, putting it mildly, a tumultuous family life. After severe dust storms hit Pampa in 1935 Woody, like many others of that time and place in his situation, left for California to find work picking vegetables or fruit. By now their first child, Gwen, was born. His first venture to California was short; Woody returned to Pampa and their second child, Sue, was born. Returning to California in 1937 things fared better. Woody was able to use his musical talents to get a radio show with Maxine "Lefty Lou" Crissman, and he sent for Mary and their two children to join him. Their third child, Will Rogers Guthrie, was born in Los Angeles. All well and good so far: Woody leaves home in Texas to find work and support his family. He is able to do so and sends for his family to join him. But all well and good really wasn't so all well and good.

It was roughly during the same time frame that Woody was settling his family in the Los Angeles area that he became sensitized to the plight, and the unconscionable exploitation, of the farm workers. This led him to develop the strong social conscience that would stay with him for the rest of his life. He became good friends with Ed Robbin, a writer for the *People's Daily World* and a strong union organizer, and his wife Clara. Ed and Woody quickly became comrades in arms in the struggle for social and economic justice for working people.

Here's the paradox again: As Woody took up the righteous cause of exploited workers, both with his songs and with his immersion in the labor movement, the "cause," so to speak, of his family was often left unattended and sadly compromised. Another passage from Ed Cray's *Ramblin Man* captures the dichotomy well:

"At times Mary and the two girls [Will was not yet born] joined Woody and the Robbin family on trips to the beach. Most of the time Guthrie came alone to the Robbin home and stayed as long as he liked. So far as Ed Robbin could tell Mary seemed to accept it; after all, she said, 'that's what men did.' Others were not as tolerant. Norman Pierce, a Democratic Party worker responsible for organizing the unemployed, judged Guthrie talented, but 'a cocksman' who used music to seduce girls. 'Woody [Pierce said] was a great lover of humanity, but he was rough on people individually.'"(6)

Rough or not the marriage continued on, and landed in another apparently secure place a few short years later. In 1940 Woody left Los Angeles for New York, largely at the impetus of actor Will Geer who had become another comrade-in-arms with Woody in the labor struggle. When Geer landed a role in the Broadway play *Tobacco Road* he convinced Woody to join him in the Big Apple. Mary and the three children went back to Pampa to await the outcome. This was when Woody met Pete Seeger and the others who would become the Almanac Singers. It was also when he hit financial success with a coast-to-coast radio show, *Pipe Smoking Time* sponsored by Model Tobacco, as described in an earlier chapter. He brought Mary and the kids to New York City while riding a wave of cash. Once again, all seemed well.

But it was a very short lived wave. Woody may well have felt he was standing on principle when he, in effect, told the Model Tobacco people where they could put the money they were paying him after he refused to accept the restrictions they tried to enforce as to what he could and could not sing on the air. It was, in fact, a principled stand; but, again, it came at the expense of his family.

The financial security in New York quickly gave way to a return to an open-ended vagabond life as Woody, Mary, and the three children piled in a car and drove back to Los Angeles, even though Woody had no job prospects there. They reconnected with the Robbins, but all was far from well. Whatever connections Woody may have thought he still had back in L.A., they came to naught. Again, Ed Cray describes the scene:

"In a fit of beer-born depression one Saturday afternoon Guthrie began heaving empty beer bottles through the windows of the house (they had rented). Amid the sound of breaking glass Mary and the frightened children fled to the Robbins home . . . The drinking got worse and worse according to Ed Robbin. Guthrie would spend time in Skid Row bars singing for nickels and pennies, drinking the night away. Mary was miserable. 'She didn't know what to do,' Clara Robbin said. Mary and Woody argued more often, more heatedly. During one spat Woody slapped Mary. 'She was not looking for the kind of thing Woody was looking for,' said Seerna Weatherwax, who with her husband Jack, befriended the Guthries (in) 1941. 'Mary was very nice, but a rather simple woman. She wanted a home for her family but her husband could not stay put.'"(7)

Still, another upturn came later that year when Woody got an offer from the Department of Interior to write songs for a documentary the Department was making about the Grand Coulee Dam in the Pacific Northwest. So, it was off to Portland, Oregon with the whole family in tow. Woody wrote some marvelous songs on this trip, the best known being "Roll on Columbia." But, once again, the stability and well-being of his family was incidental. In June of 1941 Woody took off on a nationwide tour with the Almanac Singers, and Mary and the children were left to more or less fend for themselves. They moved back to Los Angeles to wait for Woody and the Almanac Singers to meet them there after the tour.

But by now the marriage was over. Mary took the children back to Texas for good. She and Woody divorced two years later. Mary later remarried and became Mary Boyle. Gwen and Sue, very tragically, died of Huntington's Disease. Will was killed in an automobile accident while he was in his twenties. Mary took an understanding and forgiving attitude towards her one-time husband in the latter years of her life. In an article for a Pampa newspaper in October of 1993 she said, "I have no regrets. There were good times and bad times together. My brother [Matt Jennings] said Woody was never the type that should have been a husband. He just wanted to conduct his own life at his pace (and) in his lifestyle."(8)

"Never the type" or not Woody wasn't finished with marriage and family life. In was just a little over a year from his parting ways with Mary, and back in New York once again, when Woody met Marjorie Greenblatt Maiza. Her marriage to Joseph Maiza notwithstanding, they commenced an affair that resulted in—along with the end of Marjorie's marriage—the birth of a daughter, Cathy, in February of 1943. Woody and Marjorie would eventually marry in November of 1945 and settle in Brooklyn, New York.

As seen in an earlier chapter, the most heart-wrenching chapter in Woody and Marjorie's life was the horrible death of four year old Cathy in an apartment fire in February of 1946. As also seen in that earlier chapter, some of the most poignant pieces of writing from Woody Guthrie are found in the letters of reply he wrote to his many friends and loved ones who had expressed their condolences to him and Marjorie following Cathy's death.

Writing those letters, however, was not the only way Woody dealt with the loss of Cathy. He also fell into some of his, by now, well trod patterns of destructive behavior. A few weeks after Cathy's death Woody accepted an invitation from the Bonneville Power Authority to come back to Spokane, Washington to sing at a convention they were holding. He cashed in his plane ticket and took to the highway, heading for the Pacific Northwest, but stopping over in Pampa. Ed Cray picks up the story:

"(Woody) sought solace in familiar towns along the way among old friends and family. In Pampa the town was little changed . . . He told his old friend John Gikas that he had no plans, he was heading for the coast. Gikas put Guthrie up. For the next two

weeks Guthrie 'spent a lot of time' (Gikas' words) at the home of
Kate Heiskel. While Mrs. Heiskel was a fan of Guthrie's and one
of the few in town who had his RCA records, Guthrie was more
interested in her daughter, Deaun, (who) 'was a runaround girl.'
And if Deaun was busy there were the 'raunchy' waitresses at
the Empire Café just below Gikas' apartment. (As Gikas noted),
'Guthrie would chase anything. For a few weeks Woody was like
a sailor ashore.'"(9)

He did make the gig in Spokane and worked his way back to
New York by way of Los Angeles where he sought to reconnect with
Maxine Crissman, his radio partner from his earlier days in L.A. By
now Maxine was married and had a three year old daughter—close
to the same age Cathy had been at her death. Whatever Woody's
intentions on this visit may have been, the only lasting outcome of it
was Maxine's awareness that something simply was not right with
her one-time singing companion: "He wasn't Woody. He looked
very, very bad. I didn't know him at all."(10)

Ms. Crissman's observation points to the very fuzzy territory
one gets into when it comes to assessing Woody Guthrie's behavior,
and the way he lived his life in general, from the late 1940s onward.
How much of it is Woody being Woody in the manner that his first
wife, Mary, saw and experienced; and how much of it is indicative of
the early symptoms of Huntington's Disease as they began to appear
in his life towards the close of the decade? There is, of course, no
hard and fast line between the two, as Woody moved into the phase
of his life when Huntington's gradually began to overtake him.

His mother, Nora Belle, had begun showing early signs of the
malady around the time she turned 30; and died at age 42. Woody
was 34 years old (1946) when Lefty Lou noticed that "He wasn't
Woody." Ironic as it may be, it was during the time of these early
manifestations of Huntington's Disease that Woody and Marjorie had
three more children following the death of Cathy—Arlo Davy, Joady
Ben, and Nora—all who whom, blessedly, have escaped the disease.

Two instances from this part of Woody's life, among many that
could be cited, point to the fuzzy territory just mentioned. Some of
his writings around this time took on an explicitly sexual nature. A

certain level of ribaldry—let's say—can be found in a fair amount of Woody's writings, particularly in his book *Seeds of Man*. But what had been, basically, sexual playfulness began to take a harsh and even violent turn. In 1948 he wrote a series of letters to Maxine Crissman's younger sister, Mary Ruth, at a time when she (Mary) was seeking a divorce and he (Woody) was in one of his several estrangements from Marjorie. From *Ramblin' Man:*

"There were as many as twelve rambling letters, typed on legal sized foolscap with handwritten comments in the margins. Guthrie wrote in passionate detail how he would make love to Mary Ruth, going on for pages. Into the envelopes Guthrie stuffed pages torn from New York's tabloids with magenta circles slathered around stories of grisly murders. The packets frightened Mary Ruth by their intensity, the sexual proposals, and the suggestion of violence. She drove to Los Angeles to show them to her sister, who knew Guthrie best of all. 'You have no idea how horrible it was,' her older sister Maxine said. She, in turn, called the police."(11)

The upshot of the whole episode was that Woody was arrested and tried in New York City, under the Comstock Act. Thanks to representation by his lawyer and former Merchant Marine buddy, Jim Longhi, Woody avoided jail by offering to get psychiatric counseling for a "sexual behavior disorder."(12). Such charges, most likely, would not hold up today. But however specious his legal culpability may have been, Woody's expressive behavior was taking an increasingly bizarre and troubling turn.

A far more bizarre turn, however, was his relationship with Anneke Van Kirk, a very attractive and musically talented young woman whom Woody met in 1952 on another of his trips to California. By now he'd already been hospitalized, off and on, and had been diagnosed with Huntington's Disease. Even so, Woody got a Mexican divorce from Marjorie in October of 1953 so he could marry a pregnant, by him, Anneke. Their road ramblings took them from living on Will Geer's property north of Los Angeles to Florida, and points between. In January of 1954 they wound up back in New York where their child Lorina Lynn was born—and later given up for adoption.

The following year, 1955, Woody checked himself back in to Brooklyn State Hospital, where he'd been before. This time, however, it turned out to be continuous hospitalizations for Woody Guthrie—with some occasional releases—until his death in 1967. He and Anneke were divorced in 1955. By now Marjorie had become remarried to Al Addeo, but her loyalty to Woody remained steadfast. She took the three children to visit their father. She kept in touch with him as Woody's work was discovered and sung and celebrated by the generation that came of age in the 1960s, including a young and aspiring poet, songwriter, and musician, Bob Dylan. Following Woody's death Marjorie Greenblatt Maiza Guthrie Addeo founded the Committee to Combat Huntington's Disease, which has now become the Huntington's Disease Society of America. She died in 1983.

We come back to the holy paradox. No moral judgments are intended in anything that's been written here. Woody lived both the life he chose as well as the life that was chosen for him at the moment of his conception. The two, as already noted, cannot be cleanly broken out into separate components. Woody Guthrie, as I've come to see his life, was one of those individuals who was simply unable to cut the deal with life that most of us make. Mary Jennings apparently figured that out; and Marjorie probably did too; as, I would imagine, did most of those persons who loved the man that they also found hard to like at times.

The deal most of us cut is that we live well ordered lives and play by the rules (yes perhaps allowing ourselves a little edginess now and then) in return for the kind of safety and security that we human beings, most of us that is, need in order to make it through our lives. It's a perfectly good deal for those who can make it. It's given my life its share of satisfaction and enjoyment.

But to encounter, either personally or through some other type of knowledge, someone who lives beyond The Deal can generate feelings of awe and envy on the one hand, and disgust or even anger on the other. We want to be like them and thank God we're not like them, practically all in the same breath: Wow, wouldn't it be great to be like Woody Guthrie out there riding the rails, and standing up for the working man, and writing all those great songs and having his pick of women wherever he went. And, then, wow, I'm sure glad I'm not like Woody Guthrie who treated women like disposable commodities, went somewhere beyond being unfaithful to his wives, and was a general pain in the ass to those who cared about him the most.

Both "wows," however, are more caricature than they are reality. I can't get inside the man's head or heart or soul but somewhere in the depth of his being, I'm going to guess, Woody Guthrie must have experienced a struggle between wanting to truly express his love and care for those who loved and cared about him the most, even as other of his impulses pulled him away from that same love and care he so dearly wanted to share.

I believe Woody Guthrie struggled with the same question as did Gandhi and Jesus, as cited earlier: "Who is my family?" It likely was a painful struggle for Woody to face this question, however consciously he asked it of himself or not. He felt a mystical link to a greater human family even as he surely knew he was coming up short with the families who needed him the most. He loved deeply while struggling to show his love for those who personally needed it the most. Artistic creativity, more often than not, grows out of, or is a response to, emotional pain. How many of Woody's wonderful songs and poems grew out of a painful emotional and psychological and spiritual struggle he was having with the contradictions he found within himself?

The sacred is so often found in the broken. The holy often hides in the shadow side of our lives. One of my poet friends, and a former colleague in the liberal ministry, the late Rev. Ric Masten has put it this way in his song *Let It Be A Dance*:
the morning star comes out at night.
without the dark there can be no light.
and if nothing's wrong then nothing's right.
so let it be a dance.(13)

Such was the sacred dance that was the life of Woody Guthrie.

CHAPTER EIGHT

Seeking the Spirit in the Final Years

No Help Known

Huntington's chorea
Means no help known
In the science of medicine
For me
And all of you choreaites like me
Because all my good nurses
And all my good medicine men
And all my good attendees
All look at me and say
By your words and by your looks
Or by your whispers
There's just not no hope
Nor not no treatments known
To cure me of my dizzy [illegible]
Called chorea

Maybe Jesus can think
Up a cure of some kind.(1)

Woody wrote this touching poem in November of 1954 while in Brooklyn State Hospital. It's written in scrawled pencil on a yellow lined pad. Some two years after this piece of writing Woody would find it difficult to write at all, even though his death would not come until 1967. But in the five years from the time of his first hospitalization in early 1952 until he could no long write, Woody Guthrie poured forth uncountable pages of letters, poems, journal-like notes to himself, and even a play. While a discernable current of religious and spiritual sentiments can be found interwoven in much of his work throughout his life, it is during this time that these sentiments become the most intense. Woody's biographers have told the story of his final years in good and sufficient detail. This brief chronology of the last fifteen years of his life is offered to provide a context for his writings of that time.

As the 1950s got underway Woody's behavior became an increasingly erratic mixture of the manifestations of Huntington's Disease and his heavy drinking as one aggravated the other. Following the birth of their fourth child, Nora, in January of 1950, his and Marjorie's marriage went into a series of on-again, off-again separations and reunions; and Marjorie began a relationship with a new man in her life, Tony Marra.

In May of 1952 Woody entered King's County Hospital for a three week detoxification program following a violent encounter with Marjorie. Shortly after his release, in June of 1952, he was placed in the psychiatric ward of Bellevue Hospital, again, ostensibly, to dry out from his drinking. He had only been out of Bellevue for less than a week when, with Marjorie's persistence, he was admitted once again to Brooklyn State Hospital. BSH had recently initiated a program of insulin shock therapy for alcoholism. Shortly before Woody was to begin this regimen, however, a young doctor on the BSH staff suggested he might have Huntington's Disease. Woody's heavy drinking notwithstanding, this proved to be the correct diagnosis. He had inherited the disease from his mother, Nora Belle Tanner Guthrie. It would later claim the lives of the two daughters he'd had with Mary Jennings.

Woody had been showing the initial effects of the disease for several years prior, following Cathy's death in early 1946, with his drinking serving to exacerbate the symptoms. But his condition at the time of his 1952 diagnosis did not, in the opinion of the doctors at Brooklyn State, call for his permanent hospitalization. He was released in late September of 1952. One of his closest friends and confidants in the ensuing years was Ramblin' Jack Elliot.

The two years following his September, 1952, release from Brooklyn State were arguably the most bizarre ones in even Woody Guthrie's highly unconventional life. The Huntington's diagnosis notwithstanding, he sought to return to his rambling man life by setting out for California to link up with his old friends Will and Herta Geer. The Geer's were living on a piece of land in Topanga Canyon just north of Los Angeles where, in the wake of Will's being blacklisted with the Joseph McCarthy Era in full swing, they were seeking to set up a writers and actors colony. Woody moved into one of their outbuildings. Among those on the premises was an attractive young singer and artist, Anneke Van Kirk Marshall. Even with Anneke's being married, and with her husband also present, she and Woody began a relationship. They left the Topanga community together shortly thereafter. After a swing through New York they wound up in Florida for a time, and then headed back westward stopping in Cuidad Juarez long enough for Woody to get a Mexican divorce from Marjorie so he and Anneke could marry. Then it was back to Topanga for a brief spell before heading east again, in November of 1953, with a now very pregnant Anneke. It was Marjorie, even though Woody had divorced her, who took the two under her wing when they got back to New York. Anneke gave birth to a daughter in February of 1954 and she and Woody parted ways shortly thereafter. A little over a year later they would divorce and the daughter would be put up for adoption. In the summer of 1954 Woody made one last sad and tragic cross country trip, mostly down and out, and spending many a night in jail in one town or another for vagrancy.

Back in New York in mid-September of 1954 Woody checked himself in to Brooklyn State Hospital for yet another stay. He would, for all intents and purposes now, remain hospitalized for the remainder of his life. He was briefly released from BSH in May of 1956 only to get arrested on the now familiar charge of vagrancy in New Jersey while on his way to link up with friends there. Following this arrest he was recommitted, this time to Greystone Park Hospital in New Jersey, where he would spend five years. In 1961 he was transferred back to Brooklyn State where he would spend the remainder of his life.

Even as she got remarried to Al Addedo, after her relationship with Tony Marra ended, Marjorie continued to visit her former husband, and saw to it that their children got to visit him as well. In something of a passing-of-the-torch encounter Woody was visited by 19 year old Bob Dylan in February of 1961. By now he could barely speak. Woody Guthrie died on October 3, 1967.

As noted, Woody was only able to write for the first 4 to 5 years of this span of time. But it was an extremely prolific time with respect to his writing, in large measure perhaps, because he had nothing else to do or that he could do. His sentiments, as one might imagine, are all over the place. There are touching references to his reliance on God and Jesus along with expressions of desperation and hopelessness over his plight. In some places he expresses his eternal love for Marjorie, even though their marriage was legally over, and states his desire to restore their marriage. But then pours forth renunciations of her in other places. At one point he says Anneke will get all of his inheritance and Marjorie nothing, even though he was married to neither woman at the time he wrote it. He writes of his love and devotion to his children in some places, and then takes them to task for not visiting or writing him enough in others. He's fighting his demons and asserting his faith all at the same time.

Much of his writings from his initial hospitalizations (1952-54) have to do with his drinking, with some of them written before the Huntington's diagnosis was made. In one confessional passage he reaches back to his relationship with his father, and tells of how he (Woody) felt he had to "man up," to use a contemporary expression, to merit his father's love and approval:

"I wanted to prove to my Dad that I loved him the same as ever, in spite of his habits of drinking and smoking too much. So I smoked too much. And I drank too much. And I cussed too much. And I sinned too much. To prove to my Dad that love can laff (sic) at all our bad habits. What else have we got to laff at anyway? I never did know clear." (2). He writes in this same entry of how he stole his father's moonshine as a kid and then goes on for page after page about the effects of alcohol on him including this: "You hate and despise your own self, your very family, your own kids, and your worth is so bad by now that you've got not much desire to live or to wrestle and fight with it anymore . . . you wade out deeper and deeper in your own hard made poison flow of alcohol. I saw and learned that hell is not operated like we commonly think it is; it is not anywhere any great distance away from here. Hell for me is just any old place or spot called a bar or a pub or a saloon or a tavern." (3)

But then comes the counterpoint—in this same plethora of writing—where Woody attempts to lift himself up. He seeks a greater spiritual connection with all he sees around him, possibly as he looks out of a hospital window. He gives this short passage the title of *Rising Up*: "I see the main work of the poet in me as the labor of lifting myself up above myself as I look where I come and go; to get out of my body and into this tree, into this grass, into this bird, into this fish, into this food and into this drink, and to tell you not to fret, not to fuss, not to curse because everything is better than you think it is; I learn my job by watching my three kids play, Arlo, Joady, and Nora Lee."(4)

He had expressed similar sentiments some weeks earlier, also at Brooklyn State, as he tried to reach beyond his current plight for that greater vision he carried with him for most of his life: "You have to aim at a higher goal in life than just enough food and enough shelter for your own person, and for your whole family as far as that goes. You've got to find some bigger way to help your own loved ones and still some bigger way to help every living person of the human race, because if we do have any soul or any feelings of any mind to speak of at all it asks us to work harder, to work better and to help more and more of our people."(5)

To look at these juxtapositions of Woody's thoughts and feelings during July and August of 1952—and just prior to the Huntington's diagnosis—is to witness an intense spiritual struggle. It's the struggle between the absence of Spirit, or the absence of God if you will, and an attempt to maintain a redeeming vision in the face of despair. It's also a struggle between body and soul. His body is falling prey to the combined effects of his drinking and Huntington's chorea. At some point the drinking will cease, even as the disease will continue to take its toll. But his soul still strives: "If we do have any soul to speak of it asks us to work harder to help more and more of our people."

Intertwined within this struggle is an attempt to save what Woody probably knows is a lost marriage. His behavior, often alcohol driven, leading up to his summer of '52 hospitalizations, had endangered the well being of his family and largely put an end to his being a husband to Marjorie. But he's not willing to give up either. Just prior to the *Rising Up* passage where he writes lovingly of their three children he begs Marjorie not to give up on their marriage:

"I firmly believe we are criminals in the worst degree if we bust our family apart and split our family apart or do any more to make it less of a family. We've not just got a family, we've got the best family on earth when I get well enough and make it all better. You've done such a good job of keeping our family as a family that you make me believe all over again in miracles. Miracle Maker Marjorie, that's what I'll call you.

"I'll work miracles now to get healed and stay healed. I'll call on greater wonders now to give me for now and for all eternity such a sober quiet calm and happy hearted life that I'll not recognize myself anymore, my old shell, my older wild senseless self lays long dead somewhere. I, the new me, the new Woody Guthrie live only to do my human race as much good favors per hour as I've done insane deeds per hour up to now in time and endless space."(6)

As a later rejoinder to these words to Marjorie, Woody adds this message to himself, writing in Biblical-like cadences: "These things that I now ask shall be for all times and ordered and commanded (to) get me clear and keep me sober so my cold arrogance will be overcome and my silly pride forgotten."(7)

As the summer of 1952 gave way to fall Woody's spirits continued to alternate between desperate lows of self-pity and a reaching for hope and newness of life. On one mournful September day he writes: "I feel today like I never want to write another song. I don't want to ever play any more music. I don't want to write another word on useless paper. It didn't do us any good did it? All my crazy labors didn't help one ounce . . . I guess this must be my morning to pity poor old Woody."(8)

But then it is one of his children who provide him the antidote to being poor old Woody: "Hospital—Hopetal. I heard Joady pronounce it without the 's' and he put in an 'e' to make it 'hopetal' or h-o-p-e-t-a-l. He leaves out the 's' and puts the hope back in, so the institution's main job and public function will be to put all our lost hopes back into perfect condition."(9)

He invokes his wife and children in a 29 line poem, also written at this same time, which he titled *Power in My Sky*. These are just a few of the lines:

Cure me, cure me.

Give me my Arlo now

Give me my Joady/Puffey [Nora]

Forgive me my brutal action

Take all my sins away

Keep Marjorie true to me.(10)

While one day he's saying he never wants to write another song, at another point at this approximate same time Woody asks, "What language will we speak when we get up to heaven? I'd say the language of singing and the dialect of dancing."(11)

Woody's first round of hospitalizations came to an end in this month of September of 1952 once he'd dried out from his latest bout with alcohol and had finally, and properly, been diagnosed with Huntington's Disease. For all of his importuning to Marjorie to preserve their marriage, and for all the genuine love and affection he expressed for his children, and for all of his presumably sincere attempts to be "Rising Up" or reaching for "Power in the Sky," once released from Brooklyn State Hospital Woody embarked upon the brief but bizarre "Anneke Van Kirk Stage" of his life, as already described.

Two years to the month (September) later he would be back in Brooklyn State Hospital in September of 1954. In those two years, as seen earlier in this chapter, he met Anneke, divorced Marjorie, and had a child by Anneke who was later put up for adoption. Marjorie began a relationship with Al Addeo, and they would eventually marry. Woody and Anneke would later divorce. Much of the bizarreness of those two years can, of course, be attributed to the increasingly intense effects of Huntington's Disease on Woody Guthrie. He would spend the remainder of his life, from September of 1954 on, coping as best he could with his continual physical debilitation as it took its excruciatingly slow pace for another 13 years.

The poem cited at the beginning of this chapter points to Woody's increasing reliance, beginning in the fall of 1954, on the religion to which he was first exposed. He may well have "liked them all," and been notably knowledgeable in a wide range of the world's religious faiths, but now it's Jesus who gets the lion's share of his attention when it comes to seeking spiritual solace. In December of 1954, with—quite likely—symbols of the birth of Jesus in view. Woody wrote *Jesus My Doctor*. The sub-heading reads, "Words and Music by me Woody Guthrie." Perhaps he had a tune in his head, maybe that of an old gospel hymn; but one that he was never able to set down to actual music. The lyrics, in part, read:

> *Christ you're still my best doctor*
> *Jesus you're still my best doctor*
> *Christ you're still my best doctor*
> *You can cure what ails me.*
> *Jesus Jesus Jesus Jesus*
> *Jesus Jesus Jesus Jesus*

Jesus Jesus O' My Jesus
You cured all that's worried me.(12)

[Lyrics by Woody Guthrie. © Copyright WOODY
GUTHRIE PUBLICATIONS, INC. All rights reserved.
Used by permission.]

Using the play on words he'd gotten two years earlier from his son Joady, Woody signs off on this poem with: "Woody Guthrie Brooklyn State Hopetal December of 1954." On the last day of 1954 he adds this: "God is my best doctor. Jesus is my best teacher in every word of every known and unknown subject anywhere to be located yet."(13)

There are also journal type entries that Woody makes during this same period of time which speak to his determination to maintain a positive spirit even as he knows his fate: "I'm hit hard with my same old dizzy chorea like my mommy had, and I'm hit by this stiffering burnt arm and hand like my pawdaddy."(14) The back story for that last phrase is that in June of 1953 Woody had badly burned his arm, using kerosene to get a fire going, while he and Anneke were staying in Florida. The incident was reminiscent of a similar fire accident and injury his father had suffered back in Okemah.

He follows with this: "I just stand here and I say that if there's not any godly father above me then my humanly life (unintelligible) just isn't worth living. My mother father God's words and all of his Godly goodly promise to me are all that makes me keep on walking and keep on going along here thru all of my days and all of my nights here."(15)

He compares his fate to those he sees around him: "I came up here to my Brooklyn State Hospital and I seen so many hundreds and so many thousands of other patients around here all bitten all smitten . . . so much worse than me that I thank my God that I'm not smitten any worser, and I'm thankful to boot because God has turned out to be as good a doctor and as good a healer as I've seen anyplace I've walked thru in my old forty and eight here. And to travel into his great big high holy heaven where he's bound to cure me all up and to heal me back whole once more better than a brand new fifty-five model."(16)

The latter reference is probably to the 1955 car models that would have just come out then. The "old forty and eight" may be a reference to an older, and presumably more worn down model car to which Woody is drawing an analogy to his own condition. (His age was only 42 when he wrote this.) The passage does demonstrate a certain playfulness of spirit that Woody was able to maintain even as his condition became increasingly dire.

But then Woody goes from these sentiments to a kind of peaceful resignation where he sees his "departure from my physical body" to be a "grand good trip." Here's the passage: ""I most gladfully do bear all my ills and all my ails and all my defects and my deformities and all my cripplings and my sickness which my good great Father in Heaven sees fittin to bless my soul's body here and yonder and everywhere in my spirit's deep silence which does make my death and my departure from my physical body such a grand good trip to me and such a welcome thing to my soulful spirit."(17)

It is difficult, if not downright impossible, to look at the vast mosaic of Woody Guthrie's writings, both from his initial hospitalizations in early 1952, and following his re-admission to Brooklyn State Hospital in the fall of 1954, and find a completely definitive indication as to the state of his soul and spirit. As might well be expected, he's in different places at different times.

If we move ahead now to the upper end of the time frame in which he was still able to write, we find the same fluctuation of mood and spirit in his letters and writings from Greystone Park Hospital in New Jersey. October of 1956 seems to have been an especially productive time for Woody when it came to letter writing. In a letter to his family, with the salutation "Dearest All" he seeks reassurance of their love and care for him: "I am still here . . . I love alla you do alla you love me? I feel my jerkin chorea a little bit more and I feel my alcoholism a little bit less . . . O god just let me go down in purey peace with no complaints. I love you all, you all love me, please write, visit, come see." (18)

This was part of a spate of letters that were written several months after Woody made his last public appearance at a concert in his honor held at New York's Pythian Hall in March of 1956. From his balcony box seat Woody was able to acknowledge the loving response of the audience after various groups and soloists had sung many of his songs, but he did not speak.

Woody's correspondence with Marjorie in the fall of 1956 goes from adoration to near cruelty in places. They are, as already noted, no longer married and Marjorie is married to Al Addedo. In one he writes: "It takes a strong soul like you are Marjorie . . . you did live with me through my daily worker days and all my Almanac singing days, all the Merchant Marine days. You stuck with me in all my Army days. I am stickin by you just as long as I've still got myself any drop of life left. My soul still cries to you."(19)

But these sentiments take a sad and painful turn, also in the latter months of 1956. In an undated piece written on a paper towel is this, "Spare me my worst agony and my worst pain. I feel worstest in your presence. No more letters from you. No more . . . miserable visits. Woody."(20) In still another letter to Marjorie at this time: "I'm asking you Maryreem to write me up some kind of legal notice letter of some sort givin alla my moneys over the First Church of Christ Scientist—Boston, Massachusetts over and above any sum stated to you to help care for you and our own world shakers."(21) It's not clear who the "world shakers" are here—possibly the children.

The letter that seems to hit bottom for Woody, is one to Marjorie that reads: "I'll have to report here my past two or three letters to you to make sure you get one of them at least and to make sure my little words soak into you soul good:

No more meetings
No more letters
No more friend
No more helper
No more car rides

No more battles

No more fites

Bye baby—Woody

Further down he adds: "Anneke gets my $$ You don't get a penny"

And then at the bottom, in parenthesis: "(My God, My God, Why Hast Thou Forsaken Me.)"[22]

Spiritually speaking, Woody seems to have hit complete rock bottom here. But then he picks up again. Although undated, the next letter in the Archive file right after the one cited above reads: "Me 'n you and all of our four kids is more eternally blest by God's best hand than almost any other family of alla my people."[23]

The writings cited in this chapter are a relatively small sample of Woody's total output between 1952 and 1956. But it is, I feel, a reliably representative sample. A good sized book could actually be produced just using the material Woody wrote, for as long as he was able, from 1952 on. Such a book, however, is beyond the scope of this work.

If there is one constant in his writings of this time, however, it is Woody's quest and determination to continue living a meaningful life no matter how low his spirits sink at times. On the surface such a statement may not sound particularly profound in that we all—for the most part—attempt to live meaningful lives. But the existential challenge Woody is dealing with here is how to live meaningfully in the face of absurdity. Whatever his personal failings may have been—and they have been cited in this work—he was left, at the end of his life, to deal with a condition that was programmed into him at the moment he was conceived. However hurtful some of the choices he made in the course of his life were to others, he was finally left with a kind of life that he did not choose. It was a life, instead, that was tragically chosen for him. This is what is meant by the reference to the "face of absurdity."

Woody Guthrie did not back down in the face of the absurdity of his final years. While he had his moments of despair and resignation, as well as his times of anger, he also reached beyond these feelings for the wellsprings he needed to sustain him. Granted there is an element of desperation at times in his reaching, but there is something very genuine and authentic about it as well. He gives good indication that he felt his life was ultimately a part of a Reality with a capital 'R' that was greater than himself, and in whose care he would ultimately rest. He ends up relying on the traditional religious language he learned in his earliest years to speak and write of this Greater Reality: God, Jesus, Jesus Christ, Jesus of Nazareth, etc. But I get the sense he was reaching beyond the language as well.

At an earlier time in his life, as he tells us in *Born to Win*, Woody said that Love was the only God he knew. It's not really possible to know if he was making a conscious connection between his equating of Love and God a number of years prior to his hospitalizations, and the God to whom he constantly refers as Huntington's Disease has its way with him. But maybe somewhere in the conscious or unconscious part of his mind and spirit Woody Guthrie was seeking a Love that was greater and stronger than all the forces that were slowly eating away at his earthly life.

There's an African American spiritual of unknown authorship whose first verse sums up well Woody's strivings in his final years. It also reflects his assertion that Love is the only God he knows:

> *There is more Love somewhere*
> *There is more Love somewhere*
> *I'm a-gonna keep on 'till I find it*
> *There is more Love somewhere.*

CHAPTER NINE

Woody's "Bibels"

A long with all the correspondence Woody wrote between 1954 and 1956 he also produced two "Bibles.". Literally, the word "bible" simply means book; and the two pieces of writing Woody creates, spelling it both "bibel" and "bible," come close to being books of their own. The two works are titled *My Bible (Bibel)* and *Forsaken Bibel*. The latter is a play written in September of 1956 with the characters and content drawn from Woody's acquaintances and experiences at Greystone Park Hospital. The former, *My Bible,* is a long series of Psalm-like stanzas each beginning with the words "My bible" (usually with a lower-case 'b') or "My bibel." Woody uses the two spellings interchangeably and seemingly at random.

The bulk of *My Bible* was written in the waning weeks of 1954 and concludes with the words, "Woody Guthrie. Brooklyn State Hospital. December last day of 1954." The words have a benedictory ring to them. Not only is it the last day of a year; Woody also knows the days of his being able to get his thoughts down in writing are growing shorter. His actual writings on *My Bible* extended, however, into 1955; and Woody has, at this point, about two years left in which he'll be able to write coherently.

My Bible or "My bibledy book," as he actually heads it, can be read as an attempt by Woody Guthrie to recap his philosophy of life and point to the many sources of his spirituality and his religious affirmations. Not surprisingly, given the overall nature of Woody's writing at this time in his life, the stanzas are quite scatter-shot. In some places it sounds like Woody is equating "My bible" with the Judeo-Christian scripture, while in other places it's much more a creation of his own thought: "My bible sings all of my words and all of my musical notes and sounds to all my ballad songs I ever will or ever did make up." (1)

Early on in this piece Woody gets at the paradox of the limitations of language when it comes to giving expression to what is ultimately beyond expression. He knows that words will ultimately not get him all the way there with what "little wisedom" he can record. We need language of books, as Woody knows, but it still comes up short: "My bible of course brings up the whole subject of books. And I guess to me my bibel is just another book I spin (?) into and read. I don't much believe that (the) key secret of life will be found on these printed pages of paper we all call books. My soul is not printed here on any of my printed bookey pages. My life isn't down here on the printed page. My heartfelt eternal isn't printed here and it can't ever be printed here. My thoughts aren't all printed down anywhere, and my mind isn't printable, and any kind of a thing I could ever in ten billion lifey times print down if I tried 24 hours of every (unintelligible) of days. My humanity isn't sellable to no printer nor to any publisher nor to any editor nor to any person at any place in this universe." (2)

Indeed, this is the paradox of religious and spiritual language. As human beings we are compelled, from time to time, to probe what Woody calls the "key secret of life." But language alone, as valuable and indispensable as it is when it comes to our religious and spiritual explorations, never quite gets us all the way there. Woody knew this. And while not addressing the matter directly, his observations in the piece cited above point to the basic flaw in religious fundamentalism with its insistence on the so-called "inerrancy" of Scripture. Fundamentalism essentially equates what are ultimately un-expressible truths with the language that attempts to express them. Fundamentalism, that is to say, makes an idol of religious language and sacred texts. Religious language is really a finger (metaphorically speaking) that points beyond itself to a truth greater than itself. Equating the truth with the pointing finger is, as noted, idolatrous. Woody avoids such idolatry in his writing of *My Bible* by stating at the outset the limitations of the printed page.

Having offered that important caveat, Woody then pours it on with his own biblical renditions. Some of it echoes what he also writes to his family:

"My bible points my best finger here in my hospital to show me just how God is my best healer and God is my best doctor and how it is that Jesus is my best medicine . . . My bibel shows me love is my best muse." (3)

As the pages go on and on Woody alternates between lengthy, rambling pieces to short takes like these:

"My bibel tells me how it is that love is all"

"My bible tells me how it is that my soul is so big it can't ever, ever, ever get lost."

"My bibel tells me I must bear up and try my best to carry on."

"My bible tells me all I long to know."

"My bible makes me love you instead of hating you.'

"My bible makes me treat you good in place of bad."

"My bible makes me love peace."

"My bible makes me try to hold on and to try to live all I can even when my pains and my sorrows and my miseries all try to make my living worse than death."

"My bible heals me now and here."

"My bible keeps me wise in all ways."

"My bible sings me my ballad of truth."

"My bible chokes all my hurts and my bible strangles all of my bad bad ideas, feelings, impulses and such silly likes."

"My bible sings to me out of all ages."

"My bible shows me to love birth and to love all my days of (unintelligible) burdens . . ."(4)

These are a few samples of the "one liners" that Woody attributes to his bible/bibel. What I find intriguing is that he could have expressed much of the same sentiments, given his facility with language, without framing them in a structure that continually uses the phrase "my bible." There is something about the very term "bible" that captivates Woody. While he was not, as his sister Mary Jo has already pointed out, raised in a strong religious and church-going home, he was raised in a cultural setting where The Bible (with a capital 'B' this time) was a basic fixture in most homes, including, no doubt, the Guthrie home. Beyond its actual contents, The Bible is an American cultural icon (the separation of church and state notwithstanding) that represents authority and truth. There is nothing, for example, in the United States Constitution that requires an incoming United States President to take the Oath of Office with one hand on the Bible. But almost all have done so, mainly because of what the book symbolizes to most Americans—authority and truth. For all of his disclaimers at the outset about the limitations of "printed pages of paper" Woody uses the terms bible and bibel, in setting forth his wide ranging religious and philosophical pronouncements, as a way of giving them an extra measure of authority and gravitas. And since Woody had a certain amount of cockiness about him, there could have been a little of that going on here as well, i.e. these are not just my thoughts they are a "Bible."

In addition to the short "bible" quotes Woody offers, there are also passages of greater length that point to the spiritual struggles of his final years. As is the case with his letters to Marjorie and others, the passages range from looking beyond himself for hope and the will to persevere, to a kind of fatalism. There's this passage that has a ring of spiritual bravado to it:

"My bible puts me in full order and in full control and in full command of all my starful heavens . . . and all my whirly planets here and all my skies yonder and my winds and breezes and my cloudy banks and all my true words of life made flesh all around me and my bible makes me a full master of my life here instead of a slave."(5)

He goes on in this vein: "My bible sets me in full charge of all my ages, my centuries, my times, my years, my hours, my big minutes, my seasons, my epochs . . . my bible places me in lead (?) command of my six trillion armies here."(6)

While it may be an exercise in futility to try to discern the workings of the mind and soul that produced these words as they were being written, they could be interpreted as a Great Refusal on Woody Guthrie's part. He knows the course his life is going to take at this point. He knows what happened to his mother, and that the same fate eventually awaits him. On some level Woody has to know that he's not in full command or in full control of much of anything, much less planets, skies, and winds. Is he simply exhibiting Elizabeth Kubler-Ross' First Stage in the dying process, the Stage of Denial, in the face of his impending, or eventual, death? There is an element of denial going on here, but it cannot be reduced to that. What Woody is also doing is refusing to allow his life to be completely defined by his condition: "My bible makes me a full master of my life here instead of a slave."

One could argue that these are the words of a deluded man, but that's short-sighted. They can also well be seen as representing a determination to stand and strive for a meaningful life in the face of the absurdity of death; a mode of death made all the more absurd in Woody's case in that it was programmed into him before he was born. This, indeed, is the existential challenge of living for any human being: To choose to meaningfully live in the face of one's finitude. By the time he writes *My bible* Woody's finitude has become for him very up close and personal and tortuous. He states his determination, however, to not be enslaved by it all. Does this make Woody Guthrie a deluded man or an existential hero? Take your pick.

"And before I'll be a slave I'll be buried in my grave and go home to my Lord and be free." These lines, of unknown origin, from an African-American spiritual were incorporated into a song called *Oh Freedom!* that was sung during the civil right era—by

Pete Seeger among others—as that struggle went forward. The words are also reflective of another mode of expression, the reverse-angle in a way of what's just been discussed above, in Woody's *My bible*:

"My bible is like my very life to me and more than my very earthy life here in my pains and my present fleshy body. My bible teaches me how my earth life here is bound to come to its sweet sweet end in my death that washes away every one of my aches and my miseries and all of my painy painful pains I pray every minute here to find an end to."(7)

Woody writes of how he is in "full command of his life," and then writes about how he is praying every minute for his life to come to its "sweet sweet end." The passages containing each of these sentiments could have been written on the same day, or at least within days of each other as they are found in the same run of note paper, and the handwriting appears to be continuous. On the surface the words may appear to be contradictory, but they have a transcendent unity to them. Woody is affirming his life while welcoming his death. If no longer being a slave also means being buried in his grave, then so be it. To take such a stance is to actually say "yes" to life. The tragedy of Woody's life is that he came to his stance of affirming life while welcoming death over a decade before his life would finally release him to the peace of death.

But well before he was released from his earthly life, and while he could still write, Woody had one more piece of work still in him. He maintained enough command of his life, and his pencil, to compose a play that also uses the term bible, with Woody's alternate spelling of 'Bibel." By September of 1956 Woody had been moved to Greystone Park Hospital in New Jersey, and it was during that month that he wrote *Forsaken Bibel*.

I am greatly indebted to a tremendous labor of love by my friend, Jimmy Pollard, of Lowell, Massachusetts for doing a complete transcription of this play in September of 2006—fifty years to the month after Woody wrote it. The transcribed version runs for 41 typewritten, single-spaced pages. My efforts to decipher much of Woody's writings from this period in his life, with all the challenges involved in so doing, make me appreciate all the more the effort Mr. Pollard had to have put forth to produce a readable script of *Forsaken Bibel*. [All references to, and quoted material from *Forsaken Bibel* come from Mr. Pollard's transcription.]

Jimmy Pollard introduces his transcription in this way: "Preserved in the Woody Guthrie Archives is a manuscript of a play he wrote longhand on yellow legal pads while an inpatient in Ward 40 at New Jersey's Greystone Park Hospital in September, 1956 . . . As Woody's Huntington's Disease progressed his writing took on a prosody that in many instances is clever, creative and poetic. In other instances, however, it is distracting, disorienting and highly repetitive. I have edited these sentences and passages to facilitate reading the script. I have kept some instances intact to give the reader a flavor of Woody's tone . . . I have added no word of my own, these are all Woody's words.

"Woody has crafted a literary time machine that transports you back to Ward 40 . . . I am most excited to show anyone interested that, in the face of a profound neurologic disease, Woody Guthrie's resilient spirit was of far greater measure than the challenges he faced or the losses he endured."[8]

Building on Jimmy's observations and commentary I would say that what Woody offers with *Forsaken Bibel* is the raw material which could be crafted into a play. By way of analogy, if this were a film in the making what Woody has produced would be the outtakes; the scenes, that is to say, that could be shaped and formed into a film. My own broad-brush critique of *Forsaken Bibel*, is that it's a series of scenes—some of them quite powerful—that would require a more pronounced and connecting narrative, than what Woody himself offers, were it to be put on stage.

Woody offers his play in two scenes, a "Breakfast Scene" and a "Preacher'n Scene." He also lays out a cast of characters at the beginning of the play, but not all of them show up in the text. In addition, numerous other characters do show up as the play moves along, but they are not listed in the cast of characters. Woody gives his characters, who are presumably drawn from his fellow Ward 40 patients, such names as Old Southern, Longest Tall Patient,

Roydee Rogers, Doody Boy, Freedoe, Buzzy, Oley, Old Rich Man, and Sam. Then when one gets into the script other folks like Another Guy, Bewhiskered Patient, Old Man in Front Chair, and even Woody take on roles. As many of these names demonstrate, Woody has not lost his sense of wit and playfulness even as his physical faculties are failing him.

There's no well defined plot line as such in the Breakfast Scene, but rather just the characters interacting with one another, probably in the manner that Woody often witnessed. In this sense the Breakfast Scene bears a certain resemblance to the Theater of the Absurd works by playwrights like Eugene Ionesco or Samuel Beckett. For those who wrote in the Theater of the Absurd genre, like those just cited, life was simply a series of events with no overarching meaning or purpose, and with no underlying narrative. Beckett's *Waiting for Godot* is Exhibit A for this genre. The two characters engage in an ongoing, and essentially meaningless dialogue, while waiting for "Godot" (God, Hope, Meaning, Purpose?) who never arrives. Woody's characters, particularly in the Breakfast Scene, are reminiscent of Beckett's Vladmir and Estragon. But, in a departure from the Theater of the Absurd, Woody injects himself into the Breakfast Scene as, well, "Woody."

The character of Old Palsied Man tells the character Woody that "God knocks us down so we'll learn to pray better that thank him for all my blessings. That's why he stuck me so sickly here as I am."(9)

Taking his cue from Old Palsied Man, a few lines later Woody has this to say to two other characters, Jerry and Olaf:

"I feel like givin' up my sinful miseries this minute. But I hear my voice of my god saying, 'Woody, you always followed the words I gave you. You didn't rob, steal, insult, or kill . . . not even a bug! But I had to knock you half-way crippled so you can't run ahead of all my sicklyest people who need your help. I'm striking you about two-thirds cripple so you'd be able to pray with deeper respect than any of you ever had before. As you know, Woody, I'm your only real hope here and in your eternally rent-free home heaven.'"(10)

What the "Woody" character, and by extension Woody himself, are looking for is some Greater Meaning behind the absurd setting in which he finds himself. He listens to the voice of God to find that Greater Meaning, which is that "you can't run ahead of all my (God's) sickylest people who need your help." Woody has been given his fate "so you'd be able to pray with deeper respect than any of you had before;" and Woody is reminded that "I'm your only real hope here."

In essence this is how the Breakfast Scene plays out. There are theater-of-the-absurd type of conversations and encounters between the patients, interspersed with appeals and references to God as seeming attempts to find some kind of sense in the midst of senselessness. Woody, that is to say, doesn't go the whole distance with the Theater of the Absurd. Through the voices of some of his characters, Woody is still holding out for God. In fact, Woody sees himself—again through his "Woody" character—as something of a missionary of hope and wholeness for those on his ward. He calls this endeavor "my hospital work," and it is "My hardest and thankerlesst kind of paycheckless labor but the only real work I ever felt good at."(11)

He compares his Ward 40 mates, and the mission he sees for himself with them, to his Merchant Marine shipmates from more than a decade earlier: "I'm savin' salvagin' all good human souls, spirits and bodies. It makes Ward 40 the very best ship I ever did ride on. And I did ride on boats through four invasions—North Aferkee, Sicily, D-Day and through the V-bomber raids over London. But this is a bigger battle here in old ward 40 . . . My big fight against ever' kind of disease, evey kind of damn sickyness I see to be botherin' human kind. All the other big boats cracked you to pieces and dumped you down here. My old Ward 40 takes all these broken up lost pieces of folks and I try my derndnest to stitcher and sew 'em all back together. Oh, God, I try to piece together all your broken pieces so once more you're all better'd up and all fixend up all better."(12)

And on it goes, with Woody casting himself as a bearer of hope in the midst of hopelessness. Characters like Jerry ramble on with,

"I'm just as crazy. I'm just as voteless. I'm just as voiceless. I'm just as tongueless. I'm just as helpless. Just as soulless in here." Rusty babbles repeatedly, "You doddam doddam funny bitchy basserd." Arthur blabs from seemingly out of nowhere, "No, no no don't falsify me" over and over.(13)

But then Woody comes back with lines that recall other pieces of writing he's done outside of this play, repeatedly thanking God or Jesus for healing his soul or saving his soul, and asking God or Jesus' blessings upon his fellow patients.

In the latter part of the Breakfast Scene yet another character shows up, for the first and only time, by the name of William Willerkins, whom Woody describes as a "sexy white supremacy maniac . . . about 19 or 20."(14) In what has to be the most bizarre section of *Forsaken Bible* Willerkins takes off on a 2-3 page tirade of a near pornographic and extremely crude racist screed. About half-way through this tirade Woody puts in a parenthetical note and renames Willerkins as "White Sooperemedy."

When White Sooperemedy has finally exhausted himself with his racist rant, the Woody character says to him, "I guess God's done already hit you a whole lots harder than I ever could or I ever can . . . Even if I could, which I can't, I can't punish you one drop more, one drop worse, one little drip more bad here, I say. I see that Lord God's done already whackered you, boy."(15) Woody's take on White Sooperemedy is that his being consumed by the lunatic hatred he's exhibiting is God's own punishment of him. Woody's perspective does leave open the perplexing question as to why God would visit a "punishment" of demented racial hatred upon anyone. But, if we assume that White Sooperemedy is based on an actual Ward 40 character then perhaps the Woody character's response to him is Woody Guthrie's way of trying, once again, to make sense of the senseless—which is the overriding theme of *Forsaken Bible* itself.

There is no clear delineation in *Forsaken Bible* between the two scenes Woody sets forth at the outset. About two-thirds of the way through the play a character named Charley shows up, and the dialogue more or less morphs into what Woody calls the

"Preacher'n Scene." Shortly after White Sooperemedy has come and gone Old Shakery makes reference to "my Charley the clowny down there, he's a million times more a man of god with not one single solitary penny . . . just one little crazy godly man (the) likes of a crazy clown of a fool of a Charlie down here . . ."(16)

With the backdrop similar to what it's been throughout the play, and with an increasing variety of characters coming and going and having their say, Charley's preaching becomes a pronounced motif. In his many travels across the country Woody liked to check out the tent meeting revivals he'd come across here and there. Charley appears to be patterned after these tent revival preachers with his ongoing rants, at times, about the need for souls to be saved and cleansed. It is also of interest to note that Woody's father, Charley Guthrie, died a few months before Woody wrote this play. While Charley Guthrie was not, by most accounts, a particularly religious man maybe Woody is offering an odd kind of tribute to his father by using the name Charley. There is a stage direction, coming after one of Charley's "sermons" for "Four More Wilder Patients." These patients "Dance around Charley to mock him even crazyier. All most proudly box, fight, wrestle, spar with imaginary partners."(17) Charley Guthrie was, for a time, a boxer and fighter. It is interesting how Woody references boxing and fighting in relation to a character he names Charley.

After several pages of sporadic revival-like preaching Charley meets an apocalyptic end, with overtones of the story of the Biblical Great Flood—but without a Noah or an ark. Here's how Woody sets the scene: "(Charley) hangs his clothes around his body like all my nuttiest crackers do, all backwards, all wrong, all crooked, all upside down, all hung around on him like some big mysterious miracle of a god is holding 'em up. It comes up a big thunder cloud from off here along my ocean side of Greystone Park here as Charley squints up his eyes tighter and loves his big raindrops here splashin' down against his skin."(18)

Charley then preaches to the storm: "God, I sure do love your good fine tumbling rainfall thunderin' and lightnin'.' God, make me just love rainfall drops just a little bit more, O God, just a little bit more."[19]

But instead of his getting "just a little bit more," the storm completely consumes Charley. These are the stage directions: "(Charley) stands knee deep in God's flood of waters as my holy Gideon bible floats on top of God's flood waters. Last time we all see Charley is while he stands here, eyes shut tighter and goes right on with his sermon . . . and his bible rises higher and higher on God's flood waters."[20]

In the final scene, the character Woody walks through the ward "past all my 40 sickly patients to speak a prayer at every patient he passes."[21]

The prayer begins, as most of his do, with repeatedly blessing God and Jesus and ends with these words:

"Just wantin' to thank you my Jesus.

But I just don't see why. But I just couldn't see why, your why, your why, why, why.

Your why why why and why."[22]

The final stage instructions are" "all patients pace to and fro. All rave wildly, all rave madder, all bark their loudest. Woody walks on along praising God, thanking Jesus over and over as lights fade us all down below zero."[23]

The play for all intents and purposes ends on this note. But Woody adds several pages after this with a this instruction: "Add pages where your eye sees fittin."[24]

As the reader can probably guess, both stylistically and structurally this play would need a fair amount of work in order to ever be produced and put on stage. But it would be worth the effort, I feel. For the real question behind the often scrambled and jumbled content of *Forsaken Bibel* is: Who is the Woody Guthrie who's writing this?

One way to prepare this manuscript for a presentable stage play (something I've never done) would be to have Woody as an omniscient narrator, speaking from beyond the grave, about why he wrote *Forsaken Bibel* and what the experience was like. Such a structure would be highly speculative, of course, but could still provide a viable framework for a dramatic rendition of Woody's work.

Maybe Woody would see his writing of this play, and the experiences that gave rise to it, as yet another chapter in the life he'd always lived albeit under far more trying circumstances. He does see his fellow patients on Ward 40 through a similar lens as he did many of the other folk with whom he came in contact as he roamed and rambled the American landscape. He felt a deep affection for, and a sense of identity with, many of those with whom he crossed paths. But he also treated his stopping places as just that—stopping off places along the way. Woody was always passing through, on his way to somewhere else. His was a restless spirit that never quite found a final and enduring home. On some level he had to know that Ward 40 was the last stop. (He would eventually go back to Brooklyn State, but by then he could neither read nor speak.) But he treats it as another stop on the way. His characters are yet another set of folks he befriends—some of them anyway—for the time he has to spend with them. But then he still "walk(s) on along."

That last instruction he gives his Woody character, which is to "walk on along," is what Woody Guthrie usually did once he'd spent all the time he cared to in any given locale. His physical condition now is such that he can't get off his ward, but he can still give himself a role in which he can, once again, walk on along.

And he walks on along "praising God (and) thanking Jesus." I'm cautious about reading too much into this piece of the play's instructions. Woody did not wear his religion on his sleeve. Maxine "Lefty Lou" Crissman was adamant in pointing that out to me in a brief telephone conversation we had. I do not question her. I'm sure Woody did not walk along "praising God and thanking Jesus" in continuously verbal ways. But he did walk along with a certain spiritual consciousness. As noted elsewhere he felt a mystical connection with many of the people he met, especially those who were struggling on the edge of economic survival, as well as a mystical connection to the land in which they lived. Ironically it could have been that because he was always just passing through, that Woody's sense of identity with those whom he met was so intense.

By the time he gets to Greystone, and as had been the case in Brooklyn State prior to that, Woody's spiritual consciousness was increasingly finding expression in the language of the religious culture and atmosphere in which he was first raised. This is the language that comes through most clearly and decisively in *Forsaken Bibel*. I don't see all of his references to God and Jesus as a desperate "grasping for God" in his final years, so much as they are an indication of Woody's finding a renewed strength in the faith to which he was first exposed.

The Woody Guthrie who wrote *Forsaken Bibel* was in many respects the same man who had always kept looking for a blessing in the midst of his struggles. He was the same man who believed in the oneness of all things, and who believed that we are all, as he put it in *Tom Joad*, "one big soul." Being on Ward 40 put these beliefs of his to the test, no doubt.

However convoluted the content gets in some of *Forsaken Bibel*, and however scatter-shot some of the writing in *My Bible* becomes, these "bibles" that came from the pen and pencil of Woody Guthrie are a reaffirmation of beliefs that had sustained his spirit throughout his life.

CHAPTER TEN

His Spirit Was Made for You and Me

There's a Day's Inn off the Okemah exit on Oklahoma's Interstate 40 where, for fifty one weeks out of the year, one could probably pull off the highway and get a room for the night without a reservation. But there's one week when there are no reservations to be had as the place is booked solid. That would be the week in mid-July when the annual Woody Guthrie Folk Festival takes place there. If you're not a performer, a presenter, a festival organizer, or do not have some other "official" role with this gathering of the tribe, then your best bet for lodging is in the town of Henryetta, some 15-20 miles east. You might have to go even further than that. And wherever it is you're coming from, as you come into Okemah you'll be driving on Woody Guthrie Street.

Even at the age of 15, when he was scraping by on his wits and his hustle on Okemah's streets, Woody Guthrie was a dreamer. But his most far-ranging dreams probably did not include Woody ever envisioning the day when hundreds of people from around the United States and various parts of the world, would make their way to Okemah to celebrate his birthday with music, performances, poetry readings, and just plain partying on. It is quite the amazing four to five days.

Singers of both local and national repute show up. One of the performers at the 2011 Festival was Krishna Guthrie, Woody's great-grandson. Woody's sister, Mary Jo, comes over from where she now lives in Shawnee to host her annual pancake breakfast to support the Huntington's Disease Society of America. Each evening, as the sun goes down and the temperature drops into the lower 90s, the attendees bring their lawn chairs and make their way to a large field just east of Okemah where a huge stage is erected with the latest in lighting and sound equipment. Among the host of performers there in 2011 were Ellis Paul, Jimmy LaFave, the Red Dirt Rangers, Slaid Cleves, Joel Rafael, and multitalented and multifaceted musician David Amram. During the Festival the field is known as Pastures of Plenty.

The opening night for the 2011 Festival kick-off took place some 50-60 miles away at the Cain Auditorium in Tulsa with a concert by David Crosby and Graham Nash. At one point they were joined by Joel Rafael for an outstanding rendition of *Deportee*.

It wasn't always this way in Okemah and environs when it came to honoring and celebrating the life of Woody Guthrie. One person with an excellent perspective on this matter is Guy Logsdon, who lives with his wife, Phyllis, in Tulsa. Over the course of his varied career in teaching, writing and researching Mr. Logsdon has become an authority on the history of western and cowboy music, and is a member of the National Cowboy and Western Heritage Museum. He is especially well versed in the life and legacy of Woody Guthrie, and was very generous with his time and his memories during a conversation we had at the Okfuskee County History Center in Okemah.

While Guy is Oklahoma born and raised he recalls that it wasn't until he had a one year teaching assignment in Norwalk, California in 1956 that he found his first copy of *Bound for Glory* at a branch of the Los Angeles Public Library. As he recounts, "That was the first time I'd seen it (*Bound . . .*) because I couldn't find one in Oklahoma. I read it out there in California and became totally devoted to Woody Guthrie as a great writer."(1)

As a singer of folk songs Guy was invited to perform for a Norwalk civic club. He had learned *This Land is Your Land* and sang it. He'd been receiving applause after each song, but when he mentioned Woody Guthrie and sang Woody's song, the group of men remained silent with looks of disapproval on their faces. Later in Okemah he and Phyllis sang *This Land . . .* for a small group at Okemah's Crystal Theater, and "We received no applause."(2)

It all goes back to Woody's alleged political affiliations. Guy Logsdon again, "There was a great fear of communism starting in the 1920s and it grew over the decades. There were those here in Okemah who could not accept Woody. He was never a member of the Communist Party; yes, he believed in some of their ideas and shared some of their same goals, but he was not an ideologue."(3)

Such resistance extended even into June of 1999. As Guy recalls it, the Smithsonian Institution had a traveling exhibition featuring Guthrie's life and work. A planned opening was to be at the National Cowboy Hall of Fame (now the National Cowboy and Western Heritage Museum) in Oklahoma City. It was cancelled when one of the Museum's more wealthy benefactors objected. Apparently the folks at the Gene Autry Museum in Los Angeles had no such objections and the Smithsonian's Guthrie exhibition was placed there instead. And it wasn't until 2006 that the Oklahoma Hall of Fame added Woody Guthrie to its ranks.

But by this time the tide was turning. Okemah began holding its Woody Guthrie Festivals in 1998. Guy again: "Phyllis and I would sing Woody's songs around here and other places, but Okemah was just not close to Woody. But then, as *This Land is Your Land* slowly increased in popularity and the fear of communism lessened, and as Woody Guthrie started getting national awards and attention, things slowly changed . . . I was interviewed here by a documentary crew from France. Two years ago I was at an international Woody Guthrie conference in Bologna, Italy. So Woody is known internationally."(4)

Towards the end of our conversation we did briefly discuss Woody's religious and spiritual views. Here's how Guy weighed in: "I think Woody Guthrie was very, very devoted to a God, a Creator, (but) he was not of any one faith. He liked all of them. Woody, in my opinion, followed the teachings of Jesus, but not the teachings of religious denominations. He saw good in everything except greed."(5)

Along with Guy's observations, one of the best, and perhaps the most ironic, indicator of how Woody's hometown has gone from rejection to embracing was the full page ad that appeared on the back cover of the 2011 WoodyFest program magazine. It showed a picture of grasses and flowers growing in an open field. Above the picture, in large print, are the words "Helping make this land your land since 1902." The ad was placed by the Okemah National Bank. I guess a circle of some kind has been closed when the words of a man once labeled a communist are used in an advertisement for one of the most capitalistic institutions in our society!

Less than a year after the 2011 Woody Fest in Okemah, and as the Woody Guthrie Centennial got underway, the Guthrie legacy took another giant step forward in a story that caught the national and international media, including a feature article in the Arts section of *The New York Times*. The print part of the article was written around pictures that included a large one of Woody with his "The machine kills Fascists" guitar, a shot of the Woody Guthrie statue that now stands in downtown Okemah, a picture of his sister Mary Jo, and one of Okemah's famed Crystal Theater that is now undergoing renovations.

The article itself was about a $3 million gift from the George Kaiser Family Foundation of Tulsa for the purpose of purchasing the Woody Guthrie Archives and moving them from their home in Mt. Kisco, New York to Tulsa, where a Guthrie exhibition and study center will also be erected.

The article quoted Woody's daughter—and Guthrie Foundation/Archive Director—Nora Guthrie as saying of her father, "Oklahoma was like his mother. Now he's back in his mother's arms."(6) Much of the article had to do with Oklahoma's slow but steady embrace of a native son whom it had long disavowed.

This announcement coincided nicely with the launching of the Woody Guthrie Centennial in Tulsa during the second week of March in 2012. One of the many participants in the week's series of events was musician, jazz artist, and composer David Amram of Putnam Valley, New York and a recent inductee into the Oklahoma Jazz Hall of Fame. Mr. Amram's compositions include the musical themes to the original film versions of *The Manchurian Candidate* and *Splendor in the Grass*. He has been a mainstay of Okemah's WoodyFests each year since 2005.

In 2007, commissioned by Woody Guthrie Publications, David Amram composed a Five Variation work titled *Symphonic Variations on a Song by Woody Guthrie*; the song, of course, being *This Land is Your Land*. The composition had its World Premier on September 29, 2007 in San Jose, California and was performed by the Symphony Silicon Valley Orchestra. In the performance notes David says, "Dedicated to Nora, Arlo, Joady, and all the members of the Guthrie Family, whose devotion to Woody's legacy enables all of us to feel welcome in those pastures of plenty which he sang to us about. This piece is a thank-you note to him for all the joy his spirit still gives to people all over the world."[7] This same composition was played as part of the inaugural festivities in Tulsa of the Guthrie Centennial. I was delighted and honored to hear it played at New York City's Symphony Space auditorium in November of 2009 as part of a celebration of David Amram's 80th birthday.

Among the five Variations in this composition is one titled "Sunday Morning Church Service in Okemah." It recalls some of the earliest spiritual influences in Woody Guthrie's life.

In sharing some of his personal ties to the life and legacy of Woody Guthrie David offers this: "On a cloudy afternoon on the Lower East Side of New York is when I first met Woody Guthrie. Ahmend Bashir, a friend of Charlie Parker, Sonny Rollins, and Charles Mingus, with whom I was playing at that time took me over to meet Woody at this friend's apartment a few blocks from mine . . . . We spent most of the time listening to Woody's long descriptions, only sharing ours when he would ask 'What do you fellahs think about that?' We sat transfixed as he took us on his journeys with him through his stories. Woody didn't need a guitar to put you under his spell, and you could tell that when he was talking to us it wasn't an act or a routine. Like his songs and books and artwork everything came from the heart."(8)

It's hard to know what Woody Guthrie himself would make of all this. And it's perilous, if not downright foolhardy, to try to get into the mind of such an enigmatic man more than fifty years after his death. But in the spirit of "fools rush in" I'll be foolish enough to give it a go. How would a man who made a career of shunning respectability deal with all the world-wide respect he is now getting? I'm guessing he would accept it, and for this reason: The well deserved recognition and honor now being accorded Woody Guthrie is not because of any compromises he ever made. His life, warts and all, speaks for itself and it speaks well. The recognition he now receives is really about the world, or at least some of it, coming round to Woody and not the other way around. A good marker on this point is Pete Seeger taking part in the Presidential inaugural activities in January of 2008, on the day before Barack Obama took the Oath of Office. Standing with Bruce Springsteen at the Lincoln Memorial, and with the new President and First Lady looking on, Pete sang all the verses—make that *all* the verses—to Woody's *This Land is Your Land*. Neither Pete nor Woody had shifted their ground when it came to their long held convictions. It was "the establishment" that came to them instead.

I think Woody would have been proud of his old buddy on that occasion, and would have taken a little pride in himself as well. If from somewhere in the Great Beyond, Woody Guthrie could have witnessed that scene at the Lincoln Memorial, he may have given it a wry smile and nodded his head a couple of times, and said "Maybe they'll get it after all."

Well maybe, or maybe not. The spirit and spirituality of Woody Guthrie is needed now more than ever. As those familiar with his life know, Woody wrote *This Land* . . . as his reply to Irving Berlin's *God Bless America*. To be sure, Woody well knew about the land that ranged "from the mountains to the prairies to the oceans white with foam." He'd traveled it more times than he could count. And as much as he loved his land he wasn't quite ready to fully and unreservedly embrace is as "my home sweet home." He'd seen enough to know that it wasn't all sweetness out there.

Woody's original title for *This Land is Your Land* was *God Blessed America for Me*. One of the verses, which Pete Seeger sang at the Inaugural event goes:

> On a bright sunny morning, in the shadow of a steeple
> By the relief office I saw my people.
> As they stood there hungry I stood there wondering
> If God blessed America for me.

"God blessed America for me" was the recurring line that Woody later changed to "This land was made for you and me." Perhaps the song would not have caught on in the way it did had Woody not made that change. There's no way to know for sure at this point, and the point is moot in any case. What's far from moot, however, is the affirmation that the blessings and the bounty of this land, the bounty of its pastures of plenty, were indeed made for you and me—however the "Ultimate Maker" may be conceived.

Woody's vision was of a land in which everyone felt some stake and had some share, with enough to go around for all. As Guy Logsdon so aptly puts it, "He saw good in everything but greed."

Woody Guthrie's vision for America was not bound up in a particular, hard and fast political ideology, be it communism or any other "ism." The roots of his vision were spiritual. If Woody believed, as one of his songs clearly indicates, that every step one takes is on holy ground, then all human beings who are taking those steps should be meaningful participants in our earth's essential holiness. Such was Woody's vision; he left it to others to work out the details—details we've yet to complete. The only way such a vision will ever be completed, however, is if enough of us can still hold onto it. That will take some doing. In a time when the Supreme Court of our land has ruled that corporations are people, what plainer, more direct, and more radical response can there be to this hideous decision than to say, with both words and action, "This land was made for you and me"? With the disparity of wealth between the 1% and the rest of us more pronounced than at any other time in our nation's history, the credo of the other 99% of us could well be, "This land is your land, this land is my land . . . this land was made for you and me." If and when the vision contained in these simple words is ever fully realized then, perhaps, we will actually have ourselves a God blessed land.

While Woody's take on religion was that he "liked 'em all," he was especially taken with the person of Jesus—enigmatic and shrouded a person as Jesus actually is. I think Woody would be thoroughly disgusted to see how Jesus, "his hard working man and brave," has been taken hostage by the forces of reaction and repression in this land. But he would find solidarity with those who hold to the simple and straightforward tenets put forth by the Nazarene, which are summed up in Jesus' declaration, in the 25th chapter of the Gospel of Matthew, that how we treat the "least of these" in our society is the true indication of the nature and sincerity of our faith.

It is gratifying to see Woody Guthrie's story become part of the American Story itself. There is a caution to be offered here, however, in that Woody's story and message must not lose their edge even as he takes his rightful, and well deserved place in our nation's history. America has a way of "prettifying" her prophets once they are safely dead. It is right and good, for example, that we have a national holiday to honor the life and legacy of Rev. Martin Luther King. But many of our annual MLK Day observances short change his legacy by focusing almost entirely on the closing lines of his "I Have a Dream" speech. Inspiring and uplifting as those words of Dr. King's are, the greater meaning of his life is far from completely contained in them. Dr. King was a hard-edged, hard hitting prophet for social justice; and his critique of his country— right up to the day of his death—was often a stinging one. He spoke truth to power in ways that were uncomfortable to many of his hearers. He did not hesitate to call America to its vastly unfinished business when it comes to our ever living in a land where there is indeed liberty and justice for all. Dr. King was anything but a mild mannered minister who delivered safely soothing sermons.

And so it is with Woody Guthrie, another of our nation's prophets for social justice. As is the case with Dr. King's "Dream Speech," the true legacy of Woody Guthrie's life is far from fully captured in the safer verses of *This Land Is Your Land*, as moving and inspiring as I find them to be. I cannot walk through a redwood forest, or see fog lifting, or sit on a beach on California's Pacific coast, without singing Woody's words to myself. So I take nothing away from the beauty of this song's best known lyrics in saying that the greater meaning of Woody Guthrie's life lies somewhere well beyond them. I see two important dimensions to Woody Guthrie's spiritual legacy: One is that he demonstrated the true meaning of patriotism; and the other is that he showed the connection between spirituality and social justice.

Too often what gets passed off as patriotism in this country is more of an idolatrous, "We're Number One" kind of nationalism. Woody would have none of that. His patriotism is well summed up in those brief words in *Pastures of Plenty*: "This land I'll defend with my life if need be; but my pastures of plenty must always be free." Indeed, he put his life on the line for his country in the Second World War. Woody's was a patriotism that affirmed that this land is indeed worthy of our love, provided it's a "tough love;" provided it's a love that will only find its full and final expression when all of its citizens freely share in the bounty of its pastures of plenty. Until that day arrives then the truly patriotic legacy of Woody Guthrie will continue to be hard hitting songs for hard hit people, whoever their authors and singers may be.

The other, and closely related, piece of Woody's legacy—as just noted—lies in his being a living example that cultivating one's spirituality and working for greater levels of social justice are each a part of the same whole. A true spirituality is one that is simultaneously inner and outer directed. It is inner directed in the sense that it takes one down into his or her deepest wellsprings of personal support, nurture and meaning. There are any number of spiritual practices and religious beliefs that will do this for us. But we go inward for the greater purpose or goal of reaching outward. Spirituality is about connecting with the deepest levels of the self, while at the same time engaging in a relationship with that which is greater than the self—whoever or whatever one may choose to call this "greater than."

Woody Guthrie knew this. He said as much in that amazing letter of June, 1944 to Marjorie: "This is the highest activity of your mind, this Oneness; this Union: To see all the relations and connections between all objects, forces, peoples, and creatures."(9) For Woody there was little distinction between the spiritual Union of which he writes here, and the force and power of hard hit people uniting—in Union—for a greater and fairer share of a society's blessings and bounty. Social justice work, as Woody knew, is also spiritual work; it is about harvesting the power of the human spirit, the power of the Life Force itself, for the sake of a greater common human good.

The most intriguing four words I find in Woody's signature song are those that say "a voice was chanting" about how this land was made for you and me. It's easy enough to sing one's way right past the reference to "a voice was chanting" in order to get to the more familiar refrain. But I'm stuck on it. What is this Voice? Did Woody just need a few words to fill out a line, or was he going for something deeper? Whatever he may or may not have been going for I take it to mean that there is a Reality, a "Voice" if you will that is greater than ourselves, and that is continually calling us to our better and more holistic selves. Over the centuries, over the millennia, of human existence certain prophets, certain teachers, certain wise and brave men and women have caught this Voice; and they have attempted to bring its message to their fellow human beings in whatever time and place they were living. Some of them paid dearly for their efforts. Some even lost their lives in heeding and sharing the Voice. It was and is a Voice that says the earth belongs to all its creatures; that all are entitled to freely participate in the fullness of its life because we are all bound up together in the life of this grand and mysterious universe in which we all live and move and have our being.

Woody Guthrie knew that Voice well. He shared with us what he could of that Voice in the time he was given. God bless him.

Notes

Chapter One. *The Church of Woody?*:

1   Longhi, Jim. *Woody, Cisco, and Me.* University of Illinois Press. 1997. p. 63.
2   Personal correspondence with Guy Logsdon.
3   Interview with Maxine Chrissman.
4   Cray, Ed. *Ramblin' Man: The Life and Times of Woody Guthrie.* W.W. Norton and Company. 2004. p.371.
5   Notes by Woody Guthrie. Brooklyn State Hospital. January 1, 1955. Woody Guthrie Archives. [WGA] Mss-1. Box 8. Folder 36.
6   Guthrie, Woody. *Forsaken Bibel.* (As transcribed by James Pollard). Greystone Park Hospital. September, 1956. WGA.
7   Personal Correspondence with Mary Jo Edgmon.

Chapter Two: *Strong in the Broken Places: Okemah and Pampa:*

1   Guthrie, Woody. *Bound for Glory.* E.P. Dutton. 1943. Signet Paperback Edition, 1970. pp. 38-39.
2   Guthrie, Woody. *Bound for Glory.* p. 142.
3   Guthrie, Woody. *Bound for Glory.* p. 174.

4   Guthrie, Woody. *Bound for Glory.* p. 174.
5   Bray, Thelma. *Reflections: The Life and Times of Woody Guthrie.* Texas Printing Company of Pampa, TX. 2001, p.19.
6   Bray. *Reflections* . . . p. 20.
7   Cray. *Ramblin' Man* . . . p. 44.
8   As cited in Thelma Bray's *Reflections* . . . p. 6.
9   As cited in Thelma Bray's *Reflections* . . . pp. 10-11.

Chapter Three: *Strong in the Broken Places: Losing Stackabones:*

1   Longhi. *Woody, Cisco, and Me.* p. 113.
2   Guthrie, Woody. Letter to Lee Hays. March 3, 1947. WGA. Correspondence Series-2. Box 5. (All letters cited in this chapter from this source).
3   Guthrie, Woody. Letter to Marcia Copel. February 28, 1947 WGA.
4   Guthrie, Woody. Letter to Maria Smith. February 17, 1947. WGA.
5   Guthrie, Woody. Letter to Lou Kleinman. February 17, 1947. WGA.
6   Guthrie, Charley. Letter to Woody Guthrie. February 27, 1947 WGA.
7   Guthrie, Woody. Letter to George Guthrie. March 3, 1947. WGA.
8   Guthrie, Woody. Letter to "Slim." (No last name given). March 3, 1947. WGA.
9   Guthrie, Woody. Letter to Slim. March 3, 1947. WGA.
10 Guthrie, Woody. Letter to Pete Seeger. February 17, 1947. WGA.
11 Guthrie, Woody. Letter to Pete Seeger. February 17, 1947. WGA.
12 Guthrie, Woody. Letter to Pete Seeger. February 17, 1947. WGA.
13 Guthrie, Woody. Letter to Pete Seeger. February 17, 1947. WGA.

14 Effie Halladay. Letter to Woody Guthrie. February 16, 1947. WGA.

15 Guthrie, Woody. Letter to Effie Halladay. February 17, 1947. WGA.

16 Guthrie, Woody. Letter to Effie Halladay. February 17, 1947. WGA.

Chapter Four: *Woody and Jesus.*

1 As cited in *Pastures of Plenty: A Self Portrait (of) Woody Guthrie.* Dave Marsh and Howard Leventhal, Editors. Harper/Collins. 1990. pp.53-54.

2 Longhi. *Woody, Cisco, and Me.* p. 89.

3 Correspondence with Mary Jo Edgmon.

4 Correspondence with Guy Logsdon.

5 Guthrie, Woody. Liner notes for *This Land is Your Land.* The Asch Recordings. Volume 1. pp. 13-14.

6 Cray. *Ramblin' Man.* p. 324.

7 Cray. *Ramblin Man.* p. 172.

8 Cray. *Ramblin' Man.* p. 9.

9 Cray. *Ramblin' Man.* p. 10.

10 Guthrie, Charley. Introduction to *Kumrids.* WGA.

11 Guthrie, Charley. Introduction to *Kumrids.* WGA.

12 Menig, Henry. *Woody Guthrie: The Oklahoma Years, 1912-1929.* Published by "The Chronicles of Oklahoma." Summer, 1975. p. 2.

13 Menig. p. 3.

Chapter Five: *Woody the Theologian.*

1 Blake. Matthew *Woody Guthrie: A Dust Bowl Representative in the Communist Party Press.* Journalism History. Winter, 2010. p. 187.

2 Guthrie, Woody. *Born to Win.* The Macmillan Company. 1965. pp. 164-165.

3   Guthrie, Woody. Notes on the songs in *Hard Hitting Songs for Hard Hit People*. Compiled by Alan Lomax. University of Nebraska Press. 1999. p. 88.

4   Hill, Joe. As cited in *Hard Hitting Songs . . . op. cit.*

5   Guthrie, Woody. *Born to Win.* p. 65.

6   Guthrie, Woody. Notes on the songs in *Hard Hitting Songs . . .* p. 118.

7   Guthrie. *Born to Win.* P. 173

8   Guthrie. Notes in the songs in *Hard Hitting Songs . . .* p. 281.

9   Guthrie, Woody. *My Bible.* December 31, 1954. WGA. Box 8 Folder 36.

Chapter Six: *Woody the Universalist*

1   Guthrie, Woody. Letter to Marjorie Mazia. June 6, 1944. WGA. Correspondence-1. Box 1. Folder 50. p. 9.

2   Guthrie, Woody. Letter to Marjorie Mazia. 6/6/44. p. 9.WGA.

3   Guthrie, Woody. Letter to Marjorie Mazia. 6/6/44 p. 3. WGA.

4   Guthrie, Woody. Letter to Marjorie Mazia. 6/6/44. p. 3. WGA.

5   Guthrie, Woody. Letter to Marjorie Mazia. 6/6/44. p. 7. WGA.

6   Guthrie, Woody. Letter to Marjorie Mazia. 6/6/44. p. 16. WGA.

7   Guthrie, Woody. *People are Words.* November 29, 1943. WGA Box 4. Folder 44.

8   Guthrie, Woody. Letter to Marjorie Mazia. 6/6/44. p. 16. WGA.

9   Guthrie, Woody. Letter to Marjorie Mazia. 6/6/44. p. 12. WGA.

10 Guthrie, Woody. Letter to Marjorie Mazia. 6/6/44. p. 13. WGA.

11 Guthrie, Woody. Letter to Marjorie Mazia. 6/6/44. p. 13. WGA.

12 Longhi, Jim. *Woody, Cisco, and Me.* p. 63.

13 Guthrie, Woody. Letter to Effie Halladay. February 17, 1947. WGA.

14 Guthrie, Woody. Letter to Marjorie Mazia. 6/6/44. p. 14.

15 Carroll, James. *The Boston Globe.* October 16, 2011.

16 Guthrie, Woody. *Coney Island.* January 5-10, 1946. WGA. Box 4. Folder 44.

17 Guthrie, Woody. Letter to Marjorie Mazia. 6/6/44. p.8. WGA.

Chapter Seven: *Woody Guthrie and the Holy Paradox.*

1 Kerouac, Jack. *On the Road.* Penguin Books (Paperback edition). pp.309-310.

2 Cray. *Ramblin Man.* p. 339.

3 Cray. *Ramblin' Man.* p. 223

4 Cray. *Ramblin Man.* p. 221.

5 Lelyveld, Joseph. *Great Soul: Mahatma Gandhi and the Struggle for India.* Alfred Knopf, 2010. p.83

6 Cray. *Ramblin Man.* p. 143.

7 Cray. *Ramblin' Man.* p. 204.

8 As cited in *Reflections: The Life and Times of Woody Guthrie.* Compiled by Thelma Bray. P. 111.

9 Cray. *Ramblin Man.* p. 312.

10 Cray. *Ramblin Man.* p. 313

11 Cray *Ramblin' Man.* p. 312.

12 Cray. *Ramblin' Man.* p. 313.

13 Masten, Ric. *Let It Be a Dance.*

Chapter Eight: *Seeking the Spirit in the Final Years*

1 Guthrie, Woody. *No Help Known.* November 1954. WGA. Mss 1. Box 8. Folder 14.

2   Guthrie, Woody. Notes from Brooklyn State Hospital. August, 1952. WGA.

3   Guthrie, Woody. Notes from Brooklyn State Hospital. August, 1952. WGA.

4   Guthrie, Woody. *Rising Up*. Notes from Brooklyn State Hospital. August, 1952. WGA.

5   Guthrie, Woody. Notes from Brooklyn State Hospital. July, 1952. WGA.

6   Guthrie, Woody. Notes from Brooklyn State Hospital. July, 1952. WGA

7   Guthrie, Woody. Notes from Brooklyn State Hospital. August, 1952. WGA.

8   Guthrie, Woody. Notes from Brooklyn State Hospital. September, 1952. WGA.

9   Guthrie, Woody. Notes from Brooklyn State Hospital. September, 1952. WGA.

10   Guthrie, Woody. *Power in My Sky*. September 13, 1952. Written at Brooklyn State Hospital. WGA.

11   Guthrie, Woody. Notes from Brooklyn State Hospital. September, 1952. WGA.

12   Guthrie, Woody. *Jesus My Doctor*. December, 1954. Written at Brooklyn State Hospital. WGA. Box 8 Folder 36. WGA.

13   Guthrie, Woody. Notes from Brooklyn State Hospital December 31, 1954. WGA.

14   Guthrie, Woody. Notes from Brooklyn State Hospital. December, 1954. WGA.

15   Guthrie, Woody. Notes from Brooklyn State Hospital. December 31, 1954. WGA.

16   Guthrie, Woody. Notes from Brooklyn State Hospital. December, 1954. WGA

17   Guthrie, Woody. Notes from Brooklyn State Hospital. December, 1954. WGA.

18   Guthrie, Woody. Letter to Family from Greystone Park Hospital. October, 1956. WGA. Box 3. Folder 10.

19   Guthrie, Woody. Letter to Marjorie Addedo. Greystone Park Hospital. October, 1956. WGA.

20   Guthrie. Woody. Letter to Marjorie Addedo. Greystone Park Hospital. Fall, 1956. WGA.

21   Guthrie, Woody. Letter to Marjorie Addedo. Greystone Park Hospital. Fall, 1956. WGA.

22   Guthrie, Woody. Letter to Marjorie Addedo. Greystone Park Hospital. Undated, 1956. WGA.

23   Guthrie, Woody. Letter to Marjorie Addedo. Greystone Park Hospital. Undated, 1956. WGA.

Chapter Nine: *Woody's "Bibels"*

1   Guthrie. Woody. *My Bibel*. Notes from Brooklyn State Hospital. WGA. Mss—Box 8. Folder 36. December 31, 1954

2   Guthrie, Woody. *My Bibel*. December 31, 1954. WGA.

3   Guthrie, Woody. *My Bibel*. December 33, 1954. WGA.

4   Guthrie, Woody. *My Bibel*. December 31,1954 WGA.

5   Guthrie, Woody. *My Bibel*. December 31, 1954 WGA.

6   Guthrie, Woody. *My Bibel*. December 31, 1954. WGA.

7   Guthrie, Woody. *My Bibel*. December 31, 1954. WGA.

8   Pollard, James. Introductory notes to a transcription of Woody Guthrie's *Forsaken Bibel*.

9   [Note: All citations from Woody Guthrie's *Forsaken Bibel* are taken from a compilation and transcription by James Pollard. September, 2006. The play was originally written by Woody Guthrie in September, 1956 at Greystone Park Hospital. The numbers indicated here are the line numbers in the Pollard Compilation.] Guthrie, Woody. *Forsaken Bibel*. Lines 248-250.

10 Guthrie, Woody. *Forsaken Bibel*. Lines 259-266.

11 Guthrie, Woody. *Forsaken Bibel*. Lines 300-304.

12 Guthrie, Woody. *Forsaken Bibel*. Lines 306-309; 318-324.

13 Guthrie, Woody. *Forsaken Bibel*. Lines 848-850; 860; 944.

14   Guthrie, Woody. *Forsaken Bibel*. Line 1056.
15   Guthrie, Woody. *Forsaken Bibel*. Lines 1122-1125; 1128-1133.
16   Guthrie, Woody. *Forsaken Bibel*. Lines 1228-1250.
17   Guthrie, Woody. *Forsaken Bibel*. Lines 1594-1596.
18   Guthrie, Woody. *Forsaken Bibel*. Lines1650-1657.
19   Guthrie, Woody. *Forsaken Bibel*. Lines 1658-1660.
20   Guthrie, Woody. *Forsaken Bibel*. Lines 1667-1671.
21   Guthrie, Woody. *Forsaken Bibel*. Lines 1675-1726.
22   Guthrie, Woody. *Forsaken Bibel*. Lines 1692-1695.
23   Guthrie, Woody. *Forsaken Bibel*. Lines 1698-1700.
24   Guthrie, Woody. *Forsaken Bibel*. Line 1715.

Chapter Ten: *His Spirit Was Made for You and Me.*

1   Interview with Guy Logsdon. July 16, 2011.
2   Interview with Guy Logsdon. July 16, 2011.
3   Interview with Guy Logsdon. July 16, 2011
4   Interview with Guy Logsdon. July 16, 2011.
5   Interview with Guy Logsdon. July 16, 2011.
6   Guthrie, Nora. As quoted in *The New York Times*. December 28, 2011. p. C3.
7   Courtesy of David Amram.
8   Courtesy of David Amram.
9   Letter to Marjorie Maiza. 6/6/46. p.3. WGA.